Time to Talk of God

Recovering Christian conversation as a way of nurturing discipleship

A report of the Methodist Conference 2005, with questions for group conversation

The Methodist Church

Contents

Introduction

'Wow! Finally we are talking about God...'

Chris Cornell, Methodist Youth President, Conference 2005

Seldom has a Conference report been so enthusiastically received, across a wide range of ages and theological approaches. Created by the Discipleship and Church Membership Task Group, the report addresses head on a major priority identified by the Methodist Church in 2004, about 'the capacity to speak of God and faith in ways that make sense to all involved'.

Time to Talk of God deliberately starts one stage back from evangelism, exploring what it may be about current church culture which makes us reluctant to speak about our faith, even to each other, thus denying ourselves and each other the resources to develop as mature disciples.

Members of the working group

- Rachel Appleyard
- Revd Peter A. Brown
- Revd Karen George
- Revd Barbara Glasson
- Alison Hulse
- Revd Jenny Impey
- Ken Kingston
- Janet Morley (convenor)

A readable Conference report

Written in an engaging and colloquial style, and refreshed by pithy quotes, the report explores aspects of contemporary culture, Gospel passages that show Jesus in key conversations and elements of Methodist heritage. It is written so as to challenge and inspire the individual reader and provoke lively conversation among those who will study this report together.

Even before the Conference Agenda appeared, one district had already determined, at its Spring Synod, to make *Time to talk of God* a key district priority. When someone enquired how this decision could be made before most people had seen it, the Methodist Council member who had access to an early draft commented: 'Believe me, when you've read it as I have, you'll want others to read it too!'

The resolutions

Conference 2005 passed the following resolutions:

- The Conference receives the report and encourages local churches, circuits and districts to set up opportunities for conversations about discipleship.
- The Conference challenges every Methodist to engage in conversation about what their faith means to them.
- The Conference directs the Connexional Team to develop ways of encouraging and enabling conversations about faith and discipleship.

Alterations made for this version

For the most part, this version includes the same text that Conference received. Changes have been introduced to make more sense to the reader:

- The summary and background information has been replaced by this introduction.
- 'Structured initiatives' and 'Ideas for churches', now to be found in Appendix A, originally appeared before the material in Section 7.
- The contents list, the section 'How to use this resource', suggested prayers, introductory paragraphs before each section and some additional questions for discussion have been added, along with the visual images.

September 2005

How to use this resource

The purpose of this booklet

- We want an important Conference report to be seen by a wider readership in the Church than just the members of Conference.
- More importantly, we hope this booklet will provide a series of stimulating starting points for conversations about Christian discipleship.
- Ideally, these conversations will lead to churches trying out a wide variety of initiatives to encourage intentional Christian conversation.
- We would be pleased to hear about any initiatives you try in your church, so that we can share positive stories with others. **Contact** Janet Morley, Secretary for Adult Learning at Methodist Church House, 25 Marylebone Road, London NW1 5JR, or at morleyj@methodistchurch.org.uk.

A flexible resource

- It is not essential for a group to work through the book in a set order, or even to discuss all the sections.
- However, you may find it helpful to tackle Section 1, *What do we mean by discipleship?* to set the scene. Section 2, *Talking about our faith* may helpfully be discussed along with Section 6, *Current blocks to conversation within the Church*.
- Some sections are quite short, others much longer. You may want to read and discuss more than one in a session, or you may want to take more than one session to explore a section fully.
- Detailed suggestions for handling each section are included at the beginning of that section.
- Section 5, *Conversations with Methodist tradition,* focuses on themes that have been important for Methodists. If your group is ecumenical, or you are in a Local Ecumenical Partnership, you will need to ensure that you also have suitable material reflecting key emphases of the other traditions included in the group.

Preparation

- The facilitator needs to give some thought to how the group will be asked to tackle each section.
- It is helpful if each member of the group has a copy of the book and has read beforehand the section you intend to discuss.
- For certain sections it will be useful to have copies of the Bible, books of hymns and songs, newspapers and magazines. Sometimes you may wish to use paper and pens or crayons. See the suggestions at the head of each section for more details.

Venue

- A private home can be the most comfortable venue for conversation, but it is usually not possible to break into buzz groups. There can also be a temptation to socialise rather than have a more challenging conversation.
- Some church venues are flexible and comfortable, but others are constrained, chilly and a bit tatty. Make an effort to create a sense of warmth and purpose. A circle of chairs will usually enable people to speak more freely.

Suggested meeting format

This is a suggested format for each meeting:

- Welcome and prayer or Bible reading (eg: choose one of the passages in Section 4, or some other passage relevant to discipleship).
- (First session) Talk about ground rules for the group (see page 9).
- (First session) Ask each person to share what interested them in becoming part of this conversation group. (Subsequent sessions) Ask each person to share a thought, observation or insight about being a disciple, which they have had since the last session.
- Someone (not necessarily the facilitator) introduces the material people have been asked to read beforehand, eg: by highlighting what they found most helpful, or by raising questions. Check that everyone understands it.

- Tackle some or all of the questions or exercises suggested in that section (or design your own discussion questions). Some are best discussed in the whole group, some will need individuals to take time for private reflection first, others are best shared in twos or threes.
- With the whole group, discuss whether there are actions or important implications from your conversation, which should be shared with the whole church. Record these and, in the final session, plan how to share them.
- Agree which section you will tackle next time – check to see whether any particular preparation is suggested for that section.
- End with prayer or a worship song.

Refreshments

- It is a good idea to include refreshments at some point. Some conversations (eg: the sharing of 'Emmaus moments' described in Section 4) go particularly well over a meal. Having small snacks like grapes, nuts or sweets available during the conversation can add to the sense that this is a pleasant experience.
- It isn't easy to act as host and facilitator simultaneously.
- Overdoing the preparation of refreshments is to be avoided. Often a 'bring and share' arrangement is best if a meal is planned.
- Remember to refresh the eye by including flowers and perhaps a visual worship centre – conversation isn't all words.

Hints for facilitators

The overall aim is to make the conversation safe enough for all to feel able to contribute, but challenging enough to go beneath social pleasantries and leave everyone feeling stretched. Here are some suggestions for helping that to happen:

- When people are signing up for the group, make sure they know exactly what it is about and how many meetings there will be.
- Remember that for many people it is very sensitive to talk about something as personal as their faith or their discipleship.

(Indeed, those who do not feel vulnerable in this area may still have hidden depths to discover!)

- It is often helpful to give people the chance to explore a question first in twos or threes. In groups that are fewer than eight this can feel artificial, but for groups over this size it is the only way to ensure that all feel safe enough to speak.
- Remind members of the group that the conversation is intended to be open-ended and exploratory – so rushing to firm conclusions is not helpful and may silence people.

Some ground rules

A group feels much safer and able to go 'deep' with each other if some ground rules have been agreed. Here are some common rules – try them out with your group and then invite any other suggestions:

- The group will start and finish on time.
- Everyone is committed to attend each session unless they are ill or genuinely prevented from attending.
- We will listen to each other - no one will interrupt or speak over someone else.
- We will watch out for each other and invite others to speak rather than hog the floor.
- A judgemental or hostile tone is not acceptable.
- Disagreement and searching questions are acceptable however, when expressed attentively and with respect.
- Personal information shared within the group is confidential to that group and should not be passed on.

Some prayers to use

Father, as we walk together towards you,
keep our eyes on Jesus as he walks ahead;
and, sharing that right,
may we come closer to one another,
may we hold and support one another,
may we trust and be glad of one another;
until at last we come home to you
in his strength and his Holy Spirit. Amen

Rowan Williams

Look around you, look and see
God's people everywhere –
opportunities, gifts and graces,
riches beyond compare.
Loving God, may we never limit your love,
never narrow our horizons,
never close our eyes,
for you have so many surprises in store
for those who wait upon you.

Anne Brown

Lord Jesus Christ,
you brought us to new birth;
you nurture and sustain us every day;
you promise to be with us tomorrow;
we give you our all.
We look to you that we might
walk only in your ways;
live in your love
and share you with all whom we meet.
Amen

Graham Thompson

Living God,
inform and inspire the way we look
at your world,
that we may see strangers
and notice in them the potential
for friendship;
that we may see people of faith,
observing how we can work
together;
that we may see fellow Christians,
and with them reveal the marks
of service;
that we may see ourselves, with all our
imperfections, as loved by you;
that, looking to Christ,
we may see with the eyes of his love.
Amen

Heather Noel-Smith

Jesus said, 'I am the way and the truth
and the life.'
Christ, we look to you:
rescue us, renew us, restore us,
resource us.
Gazing upon you, we
follow the way,
seek the truth
and live the life. Amen

Peter Whittaker

On all the pathways of our lives
you are the stranger walking beside us.
With gentle persistence you press the
conversation,
urging us to tell and to hear too-familiar stories
in new ways.
And, in each other's telling, we catch your word
as sudden recognition.
Christ before us, Christ beside us,
Christ between us,
Blessed are you in this moment and for ever.

Tony McClelland

God of all,
when I think I have all the answers,
remind me of the questions I have overlooked;
when I can't find any answers,
help me to know that the journeying is as
important as the journey's end;
and when I want to remain comfortable in
my ignorance,
challenge my complacency with the mystery of
your love for this complex world;
in the name of him who died on the cross
and changed the world. Amen

Graham Carter

All the above prayers were included in the Methodist Prayer Handbook 2004-2005, ***Look to Christ***. The Prayer Handbook is published annually and enables Methodists to pray with and for each other and the wider world day by day. The Prayer Handbook 2005-2006, ***Pray without ceasing***, is available at £2.00 per copy from mph, 01733 325002 or www.mph.org.uk.

What do we mean by discipleship?

'The Church expects that each one of us, young and old, will grow and develop in our Christian discipleship.'

Getting people talking

When to tackle this section

It is a good idea to tackle this section early on (perhaps taking it along with Section 2). It would also be instructive to return to some of the questions at the end of your sequence of meetings, as people's answers may have changed.

Different learning styles

Questions (**1**) and (**2**) at the end of the section are designed to get people started and they will appeal to those who like definitions. In addition to the definitions of discipleship offered, you may want to prepare others of your own, or look out quotes for people to respond to.

Others will prefer to start with stories or a more feeling-based approach, or they may be visual rather than wordy – they will particularly enjoy **question** (**3**).

People who are wordy do not always find drawing or making diagrams easy, but the exercise slows down the quick thinkers and helps everyone explore at more depth, allowing less articulate people to gain an advantage. You will need large sheets of paper, and pens or thick crayons or pastels.

An alternative starting point

Another starting-point might be to ask people to bring their membership tickets (though not all may be members), and to show them around. Ask them to explain what the ticket means to them and how they feel about the commitment of membership expressed there (see opposite). If there are people in the group who belong to another tradition, ask them to talk about any sign or symbol of their membership of that Church. Or, ask everyone to bring to the first session an item that for them symbolises their discipleship, and talk about it.

Taking it deeper

Why not invite members of the group to consider starting a reflective journal while they are attending the meetings? Between each meeting they could write down any thoughts or insights which strike them as important, arising out of your conversations. They could also make a note of personal issues or events in the wider world during the week, which have an impact on their sense of discipleship. Some of these insights could be shared at the start of following meetings.

As a member of the Methodist Church I am called to:

- **Worship** within the local church, including regular sharing in Holy Communion, and through personal prayer
- **Learning and Caring**, through Bible study and meeting for fellowship, so that I may grow in faith and support others in their discipleship
- **Service**, by being a good neighbour in the community, challenging injustice and using my resources to support the Church in its mission in the world
- **Evangelism**, through working out my faith in daily life and sharing Christ with others.

Methodist annual ticket of membership

Time to Talk of God

'Why do we have a problem talking about our faith?...We need to be more inspiring, more unpredictable, more spiritual and evangelical, re-claim the Holy Spirit. Let us speak with conviction! We can attract members, there is no such thing as can't if we are led by the Holy Spirit.'

Elvy Morton, Oxford and Leicester, introducing the report ***Discipleship and Church Membership***, to Conference 2002

The Conference of 2002 received Elvy Morton's words warmly, and then proceeded to take up most of the debating time on an issue which on the face of it might seem pernickety, namely the precise wording on the Methodist ticket of membership.

But in fact this was a matter of importance. The previous year, an experiment had been tried which linked the format of the ticket to the themes of *Our Calling* (see page 96). However, the duties or responsibilities of members had been omitted and this had given rise to a passionate outcry in the Methodist press and the postbag of the Connexional Team. In 2002 a revised version was offered and adopted, linking the calling of individual members to the agreed major reasons why the Church exists at all. This illustrates the deeply-felt concern and interest of Methodists, not simply in rules and procedures concerning membership, but the much more important call to continuing and mature discipleship that membership implies.

Previous Conference reports have addressed a number of procedural issues about Church membership, and have also made strong links between membership and continuing discipleship (eg: 1987, 1999, 2002). This report offers a primary focus on discipleship, and on one particular way - the recovering of intentional Christian conversation - to nurture this. The working group has found itself led, in its conversations, to focus in this area, and we believe that our thinking is echoed in a number of important current strands of research and priority-setting. This report does not claim to be the last word on the subjects it addresses. It offers a rationale for the importance of intentional Christian conversation, and some proposals for recovering it. It focuses on what churches can do to offer support for Christian disciples to explore the issues that are key for them, so as to prepare them to be effective disciples in the world. It does not equip people to be evangelists, nor is it a manual for the disciple in the world. It starts a stage back from this, and we hope very much that the report itself will be an effective conversation starter in the Church.

Priorities for the Methodist Church

Our Calling set out the reasons why the Church exists, namely to encourage worship, learning and caring, service, and evangelism, and the ticket of membership applies these to individual members in their continuing discipleship. This includes the calling to 'grow in faith and support others in their discipleship'.

Priorities for the Methodist Church (see page 97), adopted in 2004, does not mention the term 'discipleship' explicitly, but throughout the document there is an implicit vision of imaginative, empowered, confident Christians who are aware of God's presence, with prayer and worship at the heart of their lives, active for justice in the community, and confident in speaking of the things of God to those within and outside the Church. These disciples are to be made and nurtured in a flexible and innovative church culture, which is creating fresh ways of being Church together, and is focused on the growth of people rather than the maintenance of buildings and institutional structures. Clearly, we have agreed to try to create a culture where we intend to be and to nurture such disciples.

The Methodist Church Life Profile

The publication in 2002 of the *Methodist Church Life Profile*, arising from the very large survey of congregations, has given us a statistically reliable account of attitudes of Methodists compared with those of other denominations.

Some of the important findings from this research indicate that the vision expressed in the *Priorities* is by no means currently a reality across the board in our churches. Methodists come over as being loyal, sociable, very involved in the activities of church life, caring, community-minded and eucharistic. However, compared with other Churches they report themselves to be not very conscious of God's presence, not that keen on prayer groups (they are more likely to be found in a social group), not particularly aware of 'vision' in their church and reluctant to talk about their faith. Overall they were notably 'moderate' in how they chose to answer the questions, seldom ticking any extreme option.

This picture is in contrast with the vision expressed in the *Priorities*, and we may well ask how to move from where we are to where we hope to be. It cannot be the case that the vision in the *Priorities* is profoundly different from the hopes and intentions of previous generations of Methodists. But a church culture has in fact arisen which it was perhaps nobody's intention to develop. We need to reflect on how this has come about and what we might need to do if we want to shift our culture. It is the working group's belief that we need to become more explicit about what it means to be a disciple in the contemporary world, and to support that by developing a church culture in which it is much easier to talk about faith with each other.

What do we mean by discipleship?

We understand discipleship to be the core, underlying calling of all Christians to respond to God's love in Christ, which is shown forth in our Baptism. This calling is at the root of everything else that we might find ourselves doing or being, in the service of the Church or the world. It is a lifelong calling that continues to be primary, even if we are later called to some form of authorised ministry. It is the bedrock of our identity as Christians, as those who are 'in Christ'.

For most of us, our discipleship will be expressed and lived out in the ordinary life of the world and not in specific ministries of the Church. Far too often Christians use the word 'discipleship' as if it referred *only* to that part of our lives which is involved in church-related activities, and had no relevance to any other part of our lives. It is almost, as the *Education for Discipleship* draft report puts it, as if 'discipleship' were thought of as a kind of 'access level on the pathway to ministry'. Because of this, and because much of church culture fails to make the connections between the gospel and our life in the world explicit, people whose primary energies are expended in their working lives, in businesses, public service, schools or the local community can feel that they do not really have a ministry or a vocation. This is a perception we would wish to challenge.

'The Church expects that each one of us, young and old, will grow and develop in our Christian discipleship.'

from the principles adopted by Conference 2001, in the report ***Learning and Developing as the Whole People of God*** (2001 Conference Agenda, p. 295)

'The term "discipleship" designates the whole life response of Christians to Jesus Christ. Everything a Christian believes and does is an aspect of discipleship: the goal of discipleship is to grow ever more Christ-like in every aspect of life.'

Education for Discipleship draft report of the Hind working group, an Anglican body with Methodist and URC representation

'Just as a conversion experience, if it is real, must lead to a dynamic walk with Christ, so should becoming a member be seen as a departure point for a life of commitment, the shape of which should be constantly reviewed and revised.'

Methodist Membership and Christian Discipleship, Conference 1999 (1999 Conference Agenda, p. 328)

'Living a life in Jesus' footprints is interesting.'

Young person responding to the theme of this report

In the working group we explored our own understandings of discipleship. Though representing a range of theological traditions, there was an interesting degree of agreement. We agreed there was a sense of **call** - a disciple feels called and chooses to respond. The call is to a two-way **relationship**, where God keeps us company and we keep company with God. There has to be a willingness to **follow** - the disciple is on a lifelong journey of faith as a follower of Jesus, and must be willing to 'go for God'. The journey is **not straightforward**, but can include moving towards and drifting away from closeness to God. The aim is to become more Christ-like, **being like Jesus and doing like Jesus.** Discipleship is a discipline that can involve pain and **cost**; in some choices we make, the gospel asks us to be **counter-cultural** - how should we live, where do we place ourselves, who or what do we really serve? It also involves **discipline**; we are committed to learn, to pray, and show our faith in action. In our love of God we will also **love our neighbour** as ourselves. And in order to go on growing, disciples must be vulnerable, curious, able to live with questions, and **full of desire to learn**. How can the Church help us to be like this?

- *A disciple is an active, intentional learner.*
- *A disciple is an apprentice and a practitioner - not just a student of the Word but a doer of it.*
- *A disciple is a follower of a particular teacher.*
- *A disciple is accountable to someone who knows them and helps them to learn and grow and live.*
- *A disciple is outwardly oriented, focused on helping others learn what it means to be a disciple.*

Mark Greene, *Imagine – How we can reach the UK*, p. 22

Questions for conversation:

1. Which of the quotes about discipleship, or the points made in the paragraphs above (pages 19–21), can you identify with? Which do you disagree with?
2. What would your own definition of a 'disciple' be?
3. Think about your own life, and use the following exercises as a basis for conversation:
   - Draw a 'life-line' to represent your life so far, and mark on it the points that are crucial in your development as a Christian disciple, OR
   - Draw a large tree shape, with trunk, roots and branches. If the trunk represents your life as a disciple, think about and write in what you see as the important 'roots' of your discipleship. Mark on the 'branches' where your life reaches out to, and then put in what you believe or hope are some of the 'fruits'.

After people have had time on their own to tackle one of the exercises, ask them to share in twos or threes. Make sure each person has at least five minutes to explain what they have drawn. The others should be free to make observations and ask questions but should not insist on particular interpretations.

Talking about our faith

'We need to provide safe and loving spaces in which to share honestly the deepest concerns and questions of our lives.'

Getting people talking

When to tackle this section

If you have started with Section 1, the people in your group will already have begun talking and sharing. This may make it easier to tackle the questions about why we, as Methodists, find it hard to talk about our faith.

It may be possible to tackle this session along with Section 6, *Current blocks to conversation within the Church.* Material there could help to extend **question** (**1**).

Taking it deeper

An additional question which could prompt some inspiring answers is this:

- **Who really taught you the faith and attracted you onto the path of being a disciple?**

(Give people a chance to think and remember by sharing with just one other person first, but then let all the group hear about these saints.)

Recovering Christian conversation

Methodists are pretty good at conversation - up to a point. But it seems unlikely that the majority of us would answer an enthusiastic 'yes' to John Wesley's question. It is no longer the sort of question we are accustomed to being asked in a church context. The findings of the *Church Life Profile* (see page 18) suggest that, whereas we are comfortable with socialising and prioritise being a welcoming church, we are much less comfortable with seeking out or providing contexts of conversation that allow us to go really deep, and to 'get real' with each other about our faith, and its implications for living.

This is strongly linked to our reluctance to evangelise, a phenomenon that has been observed wherever the *Our Calling* themes (see page 96) have been discussed. 'Evangelism' is the one that makes us go a bit quiet. But if we never have searching conversations with our fellow Christians about our faith, it is hardly likely that we shall feel able to express a reason for the hope that is in us (cf: 1 Peter 3:15) to anyone outside the Church.

'Many Christians today rarely speak of God to one another.'

Mark Davis, 'Recovering Christian Conversation' in ***Walking on the Shore***, p. 22

'(We need to) provide safe and loving spaces in which to share honestly the deepest concerns and questions of our lives, to become vulnerable to one another, supportive of one another and challenging of one another.'

from an account of a Methodist Council conversation, included in the report ***Priorities for the Methodist Church***, Conference 2004 (2004 Conference Agenda, p. 127)

'Is it your desire and design to be on this and all other occasions entirely open, so as to speak everything that is in your heart, without exception, without disguise, and without reserve?'

John Wesley, question to the Methodist Bands

For some, it may feel problematic and even offensive to be asked to share what is deepest in their heart - this is private. For others it is a real disappointment when they do not feel that their church is a place where they can talk to other Christians about the issues they face living out their discipleship in the world, or where they are supported and challenged to grow. Perhaps many others who are relatively happy with the present church culture (and the *Church Life Profile* suggests that many are fairly satisfied) would discover a new dimension to their Christian life if their church culture gave them permission to move into a deeper level of conversation.

We need to explore carefully why it feels so hard to talk easily and naturally about our faith in this church culture. It is as if many of us have taken on board the perception that has been mainstream in the wider culture for some time, namely that religion is an individual and private matter, and that it does not belong in the public domain (even the supportive domain of the local church). However, as we shall explore later, things have moved on, and there are now many in the wider culture who are comfortable with talking about their 'spirituality', yet do not associate this exploration with anything that happens in the local church.

Questions for conversation:

1. Why do you think many Methodists find it hard to talk about faith?

2. How satisfied (or not) do you feel with the conversations about faith that happen around your church?

3. With whom, and in what contexts, do you in fact feel most able to open up and share what is closest to your heart? What makes those people or contexts safe and fruitful for deep conversation?

Christian conversations in our contemporary culture

'Christian people do not stand outside society ... There must be engagement with the thought-forms of contemporary society.'

Getting people talking

A choice of approach

This is a complex section in which a large number of issues are raised, and it is important to choose how you want to tackle it. Each of the themes in contemporary culture discussed could, in principle, become a session in their own right (but you would need to extend the material with your own input and additional exercises).

It may be important to tackle the whole section in order to get an overview. In this case, rather than asking everyone to work through each point, it may be helpful to split the group into four (pairs, threes or fours are fine), and ask them simply to look at their section. Beneath each section there are particular issues for Christian disciples posed. In addition to these, you could ask groups to say:

- How far do you recognise the reality of the picture painted here?
- What other issues do Christians face because of this reality (apart from the questions mentioned in the report)?

Make sure people have at least 20 minutes on this. Then call them back together and ask each small group to share their insights.

Taking it deeper

A way of extending the conversation through non-wordy means is to use collage. Ensure that you have a large pile of magazines and colour supplements, scissors, glue sticks and large sheets of paper. (You might ask people to bring old magazines with them to the session – this way you know that their own taste will be represented.) After the group discussion, give people time to create a collage about being a Christian in the contemporary world:

- First they should talk in pairs about the elements of the contemporary world that are particularly important to them in their discipleship.
- Then they should browse through the magazines, just tearing out pages that strike them as significant.
- Then they should use scissors and glue to create a collage. They can use both images and words.
- Finally they should have the chance to share their collage with the person they first discussed ideas with. The group may want to display all of the collages eventually, or have them in the centre of the room when praying together at the end of the meeting.

Christian conversations in our contemporary culture

We are all part of the contemporary culture as well as being rooted in the Christian tradition, which is often deeply counter-cultural. But we have to wrestle honestly and intelligently with how and when exactly we may be called to adopt a counter-cultural stance. Often we cannot see clearly what may be the harmful attitudes we are caught up in because they are like the air we breathe, while at the same time we may be opposing secular movements which are of the Spirit. We need to have real conversations with each other in order to discern the way to be a faithful Christian disciple in the contemporary world. Here we mention four aspects of contemporary life, and the conversations that could arise as Christians think about them together:

- global communication and personal isolation;
- work/life balance;
- pick-and-mix interest in spirituality;
- shifting moral codes.

But there are obviously many more.

'Though all Christians live "in the world", not all are necessarily conscious of the full extent to which Christian discipleship entails a mix of detachment and accommodation (being "in the world but not of it").'

The Nature of Oversight, Conference 2005 (2005 Conference Agenda, p. 120)

'Christian people do not stand outside society, seeking to reform it; their characters are formed by the social structures they inhabit … There must be engagement with the thought-forms of contemporary society.'

Margaret Jones, 'Growing in grace and holiness' in ***Unmasking Methodist Theology***, p. 156

Global communication and personal isolation

We are the most vividly informed generation of human beings the world has ever known. Immediate, graphic and often upsetting images of suffering, environmental damage, terror and war, happening thousands of miles away come straight into our living rooms via the television. Soldiers serving in Iraq can e-mail their families or create weblogs and describe events the day they happen. The immediacy of technology has itself become a weapon of war, as kidnappers present videos of their victims' suffering as a means of humiliating governments and terrifying other citizens.

At the same time, many of us live in neighbourhoods where we do not know each other at all well, and we may even fear our neighbours. Although the church often speaks of 'the community' in which it is located, in fact the majority of individuals now live their lives in several different communities. We may well live, work and worship in quite distinct 'communities' that have little or no overlap. This can contribute to the sense that 'discipleship' only applies to the separate world of the Church. In the popular fantasy world of soap operas, people all know each other, constantly bump into each other in the neighbourhood, buy each other's goods, fall in and out of love, gossip about people they all know and genuinely shape each other's lives. This may still happen in some rural and very settled communities, but for most people in towns and cities this is not the reality.

For some, it is possible to keep more closely in touch with wide friendship circles because of the improved technology now available. For others, without access to mobile phones or e-mail, the isolation is greater. All have to cope with a greater fragmentation of community life, and an increased sense of pressure and fear about the large events happening in the world which we may feel helpless to respond to. Rural communities may have a stronger sense of safety and social cohesion. Or people may feel isolated because local services such as buses or post offices have been withdrawn. Sometimes communities are divided between those whose families are local and those who have bought property recently - sometimes in pursuit of a rural idyll.

Questions for conversation:

1. Who is telling us the truth, and how can we tell?
2. Are we powerless to influence things?
3. Who is our neighbour?
   How can we discern which community we are called to serve in?

Work/life balance

Patterns of work have changed significantly over a generation. A much more 24/7 culture has eroded any agreed space in the working week, so that (at least within towns and cities) there is no shared *sabbath*. The intensification of work, and for some a longer working week lead to pressure and burnout, and a sense that even creative and satisfying jobs are demanding too much and cannot be done humanly and well. This perception is explored in depth in Madeleine Bunting's book *Willing Slaves - how the overwork culture is ruling our lives*.

At the same time, job security has been eroded. Careers are no longer for life; there is less sense that the company you serve loyally owes you that loyalty back. This has tended to lead to a preoccupation with selling yourself and your skills in order to advance a career - no-one else is going to look after your interests. This relentless 'project of the self' to which we are committed means that we are likely to attach considerable value to being able personally to exercise control in the world and to have an impact on it. Because of this, we may continue to take on responsibilities that stress us beyond enduring, and we may suffer when we are obliged to retire or step down from responsibility.

In the past, a majority of women were not in paid employment. They often cared for children and elderly relatives and engaged in a good deal of networking in the local community. The value of their activities was seldom recognised and certainly no monetary value was given to it, or credit given for the 'social capital' - the sense of local goodwill - which this created. Now it is often assumed that everyone must be in paid employment to have a meaningful identity. There is an exhausting juggling exercise to be done, especially by parents of small children. And there is also a real 'care deficit' arising, as the invisible caring and community 'glue' which women traditionally provided is no longer to be relied on. Even those who are retired may find that their time is not 'free' because they are committed to essential childcare duties with their grandchildren. Diminishing pensions which keep older people in employment for longer will increase the pressure here too.

Bunting argues that overwork and consumerism go hand in hand. In adverts we are invited to pamper ourselves in order to compensate for perpetual tiredness and stress. There is a drive to make our homes aesthetically perfect and calming, to spend a fortune on making our gardens a place of retreat, to get away on holidays that are as far as possible from our everyday life. It is not that we are frivolously seduced by adverts: the need to seek restoration within lives that are overstretched is a profound one, and getting off the cycle of stress and desire to escape is extremely difficult.

Questions for conversation:

1. Many people feel stressed and lacking in time. It has been suggested that our culture has 'a disordered relationship with time' (Kathy Galloway). How do you respond to this idea?
2. How would you describe your relationship to money?
3. Where is the space for God in your life?
4. What kind of 'self' do you feel is being fostered within your working life or retirement?

A pick-and-mix interest in spirituality

Repeated surveys show that people display more belief in God and more practice of prayer than you would expect from the size of church congregations. The *National Census of 2001* (http://www.statistics.gov.uk/census2001) included a voluntary question on religions which 92% of the population answered. Of those, 76.8% said they had a religion, and 71% said that religion was Christianity. An ICM survey in January 2004 for the BBC programme *What the World thinks of God* (http://news.bbc.co.uk/1/hi/programmes/wtwtgod) produced these findings. Out of 1,000 people questioned in the UK, 46% said they had always believed in God; 56% said they believed in God at that point in time; 67% said they believed in God or a higher power; 12% could not agree with the previous statement but described themselves as a spiritual person. On prayer life, 28% said they prayed regularly, 18% prayed at times of crisis, 23% prayed only occasionally (eg: at marriages and funerals).

There is a sense in which our society is, in Clive Marsh's word, 'post-atheist'. There is a good deal of interest in spirituality in a general way, and a thriving market for publications, therapies and retreats that address spirituality. But the doctrines, disciplines or membership of any particular faith are not, for the most part, what attract; rather there is a pick-and-mix consumerist approach. Such an approach may implicitly apply within the Church as much as in wider society.

There exists a fascination with horoscopes and astrology, which feature in a wide range of magazines and newspapers. While perhaps for the majority it is only of passing interest and amusement to look at our own star sign for the week, others take the matter more seriously. Particularly in a work culture where we are increasingly required to take individual responsibility for making our future, there may be a real attraction in an approach to spirituality which suggests that there is an overarching destiny that controls what happens to us, and for which we are not responsible.

At the same time, those of us who identify ourselves as Christian are much more aware than we used to be of other faiths such as Islam that appear conscious, definite, disciplined and strongly boundaried, in which the sense of community identity is strong. While the majority of Muslims seek to be responsible, cooperative citizens within British culture, extremist approaches gain much media coverage and are matched by similarly extremist myths about 'the war on terror' or 'the axis of evil', sometimes given Christian resonances.

Questions for conversation:

1. What traditions do you think you can learn from?
2. Are there spiritualities it is dangerous to get involved with?
3. Are there dangers in our own way of believing?

Shifting moral codes

In the early part of the last century, the accepted marks of a Christian lifestyle were very similar to that of a 'respectable' lifestyle: Sunday observance, temperance, churchgoing, no sex outside marriage. Social shame was attached to being illegitimate, a single parent, divorced, homosexual, etc. In contemporary society, respect is given to a whole variety of lifestyles. There are legal requirements not to discriminate against people on the basis of their marital status or sexual orientation, or on their ethnic origin, religion or impaired ability.

In some ways, many societal attitudes towards sexuality have become so libertarian that the whole of culture seems to have been sexualised, and there is immense pressure to 'perform' as a sexual being. In other ways, society has become much more vigilant and protective towards those who are vulnerable such as children, and decades of abuse have been exposed, hidden within institutions including the Church.

Within the Church there is not a single agreed position regarding what makes for personal holiness, especially in the area of relationships. In practice, while divorced and remarried people are largely accepted, there is currently a difficult conversation (and large silences) between different parts of the Church about committed homosexual relationships and committed heterosexual relationships outside marriage.

Other new moral imperatives have also become important, for instance concerning environmental awareness, trade justice and the conduct of war, and in recent years the Methodist Church has found it much easier to be united on these subjects.

Questions for conversation:

1. What are the principles on which you base your personal morality?
2. How can different generations share perceptions?
3. Why are issues about sexuality the ones that divide us?
4. How exactly should the Bible guide our decisions?

Questions for conversation on the whole section:

1. This section outlines four contemporary themes. What other aspects of contemporary culture do you think are important as a context for discipleship?

2. The questions posed under each theme raise certain issues facing Christian disciples. What other issues arise for you, as you seek to apply your faith to your life?

'A huge amount of the teaching we have received as Jesus' disciples is contained, not in set piece sermons, or unambiguous commands, but in conversation.'

Conversations with the Jesus of the Gospels

Getting people talking

Using biblical passages throughout

One way to begin to tackle Section 4 is to choose to start each of your meetings by reading out one of the biblical passages discussed here. Or you may prefer to use the Bible passage set for the day in the *Methodist Prayer Handbook*, or to choose other passages that have a direct bearing on being a disciple. There are obviously many to choose from.

Focusing on conversations in the Gospels

You may wish to split your group up and ask them to consider different passages. These could be passages discussed here, or they could be passages you have identified as important for the group by discussing **questions** (**2**) and (**3**) from *Questions for conversation on the whole section* (p. 51). If people discuss different passages in twos or threes, ask them to look particularly at how certain stories or sayings often arise within the context of a conversation, rather than being spoken out of the blue. What were the parties to the conversation trying to say to each other, as presented in the Gospels?
Later, bring the whole group back together to share insights.

Taking it deeper

The final story discussed here, the Emmaus road, might go well if talked through over a meal. It would be best to make this one of your later meetings when people have got to know each other quite well. You could hold a traditional Methodist 'agape' or love feast (see p. 91) and encourage people to talk about any 'Emmaus road' experience they feel they have had.

Conversations with the Jesus of the Gospels

'Christian disciples are under the discipline of Christ. Jesus' educational method was not to offer dogmatic propositions for acceptance but to expect his followers to reflect theologically on the allusive and often challenging content of his teaching, and so take responsibility for their own reaction.'

Education for Discipleship draft report of the Hind working group

'We need to work creatively to bring the Bible alive to ourselves and to our contemporary world.'

from an account of a Methodist Council conversation included in the report ***Priorities for the Methodist Church***, Conference 2004 (2004 Conference Agenda, p. 127)

The Gospels are full of conversations - conversations that transform and illuminate. Through recorded conversations about contemporary events, everyday life, and observable behaviour, we are given glimpses of what it means to follow Jesus and live as his disciple. Jesus converses with his disciples, who are often shown as slow-witted, selfish and flawed. He converses with those who approach him for help - often women who remain nameless such as the Samaritan woman at the well or the Syro-Phoenician woman, or outsiders such as the Roman centurion or Zacchaeus the collaborator. Often he is shown disputing fiercely with opponents, and arguing with the demonic spirits he is casting out. A huge amount of the teaching we have received as Jesus' disciples is contained, not in set piece sermons, or unambiguous commands, but in conversation. There is a relationship. There is humour and anger, irony and passion. There is room for individual response. There is room for mutual learning. We do not always get told what happened next - so we need to go away and talk about it ourselves.

Here are just a few stories of Jesus in conversation that illuminate what it might mean to be a disciple. There are of course many more.

You have to ask real questions

'Jesus answered, "The first is, 'Hear, O Israel: the Lord our God, the Lord is one; you shall love the Lord your God with all your heart, and with all your soul, and with all your mind, and with all your strength.' The second is this, 'You shall love your neighbour as yourself.'"'

Mark 12:29-31

Jesus' famous summary of the Law is the basis of all our discipleship. In Mark's Gospel, it is offered to a nameless scribe whom Jesus concludes is 'not far from the kingdom of God'. Usually, Jesus replies by asking another question or telling a story, but here he is shown giving a direct answer. The setting is one in which all the previous 'conversations' have in effect been trap questions set by enemies, but this scribe seems to have been asking a genuinely searching question. In his reply, Jesus quotes the Old Testament but introduces the phrase about 'the mind'. Perhaps he is angry about the misuse of the intellect that has been evident in the tricky non-questions that have been posed earlier. The scribe repeats back what Jesus has said but notes the new point by offering a slightly different nuance - 'the understanding'. You sense a real conversation is taking place at last; 'after that no one dared to ask him any question'.

Questions for conversation:

1. In what ways do you feel you are able to love God with your mind?
2. Are there questions about faith that you really want answered, but are afraid to ask?

It's O.K. to argue

'For saying that, you may go - the demon has left your daughter.'

Mark 7:29

You get the impression that Jesus particularly enjoyed conversing with people who both recognised what he had to offer and were prepared to stand up to him. One notable example is the Syro-Phoenician woman who came to him on behalf of her daughter. Jesus initially rebuffs her as a non-Israelite, quoting a rather insulting proverb. She wittily turns the proverb back on him and he is convinced. Here we have an example of a conversation in which Jesus allowed his own mind to be changed. Another example is the Roman centurion whose slave was very ill (Luke 7:1-10). The Jewish elders appealed on his behalf and Jesus was planning to visit - but the centurion sent to say that actually coming wasn't necessary; he knew that Jesus had the authority to heal at distance. Rather than being angry or deflated by having his movements arranged for him, Jesus is delighted by what he sees as an act of faith.

Question for conversation:

Have you ever felt like challenging God in prayer? What happened?

You have to want to be healed - and it can be quite exposing

'But the woman, knowing what had happened to her, came in fear and trembling, fell down before him, and told him the whole truth.'

Mark 5:33

Even today, most women would hesitate to discuss their troublesome gynaecological problems publicly in front of a mixed and impatient crowd. This story emphasises more than most the private circumstances, thoughts and feelings of a woman who approached Jesus for healing from a condition that made her perpetually 'unclean' (and no doubt very tired and anaemic). It is also an unusual incident because it interrupts the account of another healing - that of Jairus' daughter, perhaps creating the delay that means that people had announced the girl's death by the time Jesus arrived. In spite of the embarrassing nature of her condition, and the clear preference of the woman for personal anonymity, and the pressure on him to hurry to the house of Jairus, Jesus compels her to make herself known and speak her truth. We should not assume that we either will get away without having to speak up and witness to our own healing.

Questions for conversation:

1. Can you think of an example in your own life when being asked to talk openly about something vulnerable was helpful?
2. What does this story have to say to those who have to deal with chronic ill-health or impairment and are not healed?

Discipleship is going to cost you everything

'She out of her poverty has put in everything she had, all she had to live on.'

Mark 12:44

Mark offers us a graphic image of what it means to fulfil the first commandment as a disciple - it is going to cost us not less than everything. Jesus and his disciples are watching the crowds putting money into the temple treasury. In conversation with his disciples, Jesus points out an object lesson from observing people's behaviour. He contrasts the lavish gifts of the rich people (which will affect their standard of living not at all) with the tiny but total offering of a poor widow. The Greek that is translated here 'all she had to live on' can also mean 'her whole life'. The generosity of our commitment to the path of discipleship will be measured not by how much we give, but by how much (or how little) we withhold. The vignette is all the more pointed because it is framed between Jesus' critique of those apparently religious people who 'devour' the property of widows (rather than provide social welfare as the Torah commands) and his prediction that the temple will be destroyed because of its corruption.

Questions for conversation:

1. Can you think of an example in your own life when sacrifice or generosity on your part led to a sense of joy and freedom?
2. How do you make decisions about what you give (eg: time, money, openness to the power of God working through you and others)?
3. What parts of yourself or your life do you still withhold from God?

You are going to end up in unexpected company you probably wouldn't choose

'When you give a luncheon or a dinner, do not invite your friends or your brothers or your relatives or rich neighbours.'

Luke 14:12

This startling instruction of Jesus about how to choose your dinner guests (seldom discussed in churches, and even less commonly acted upon) is part of a conversation when he was actually a dinner guest in the house of a pharisee. You do sometimes wonder whether anyone ever invited Jesus twice! It is followed by the parable of the Great Feast, where it is emphasised that, contrary to popular belief, there are going to be some real surprises about who will sit down to dinner in the kingdom of God. Expected guests end up missing the feast because they have in practice made other matters more of a priority. People turn up who are far from respectable and had neither planned nor expected to be there. The parable is followed by the equally startling saying that anyone who doesn't 'hate' their closest relatives 'cannot be my disciple'. It could not be put more strongly that the company of the kingdom is not going to consist of the people you naturally want to socialise with.

Questions for conversation:

1. How socially varied is your church community? Why is that, do you think?
2. Can you think of an example in your own life when you shared a sense of fellowship with an unusual bunch of people?

As you journey together and wrestle with scripture, you will glimpse Jesus

'Were not our hearts burning within us while he was talking with us on the road, while he was opening the scriptures to us?'

Luke 24:32

In the Resurrection story of the road to Emmaus, Luke offers us perhaps the most famous and resonant transformative conversation in the Gospels. In it, the two travelling disciples are shown unable to recognise the risen Jesus until they had experienced a journey, a conversation wrestling with how the scriptures relate to what is happening in their lives and a shared meal. As Clive Marsh puts it:

'The passage is full of material pertinent to every aspect of Christian companionship (travelling, mutual confusion, questioning, scripture-reading, moments of inspiration, disappointment, excitement, Jesus present one minute and absent the next). As an aspect of fellowship, companionship means that the group of Christians to which one primarily belongs are one's travel-companions, fellow-searchers, co-questioners, believers (who may believe differently from oneself) whose own faith and belief (in the form of both questions and answer) one can trust and make use of within one's own journey.'

'A training-ground for forgiveness: Methodism and "fellowship"' in ***Methodism and the Future***, p. 102

Question for conversation:

Has there been any encounter in your life as a Christian, which you would describe as an 'Emmaus road' experience?

Questions for conversation on the whole section:

1. What 'educational methods' do you think Jesus used to teach his disciples? Which of these does your church normally use?
2. What stories or sayings from the Gospels have been encouraging and important to you in thinking about your discipleship?
3. What stories or sayings have you found difficult to understand or apply to your life?

'Jesus, confirm my
heart's desire,
To work, and speak,
and think for thee;
Still let me guard
the holy fire,
And still stir up
thy gift in me.'

Conversations with Methodist tradition

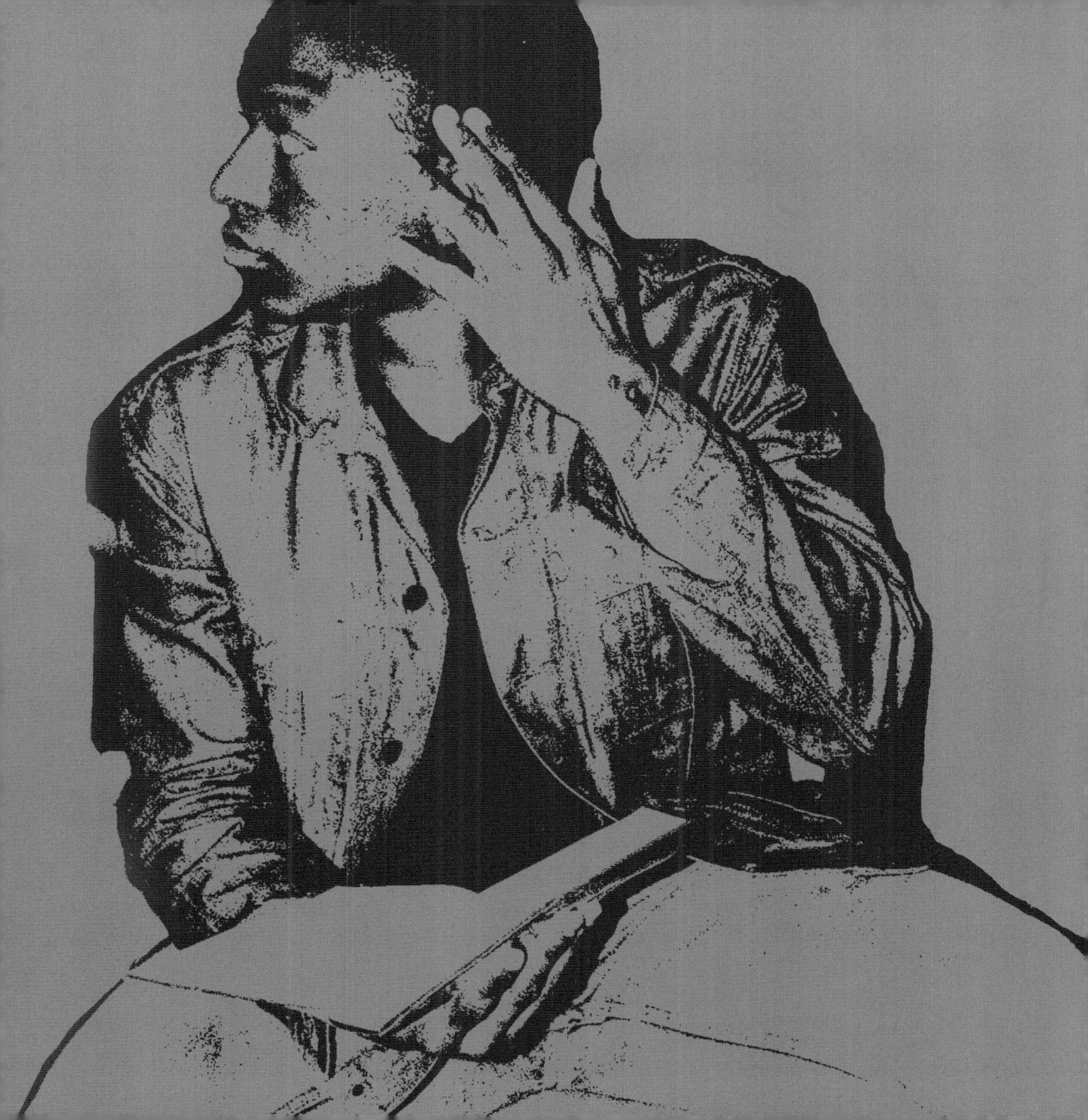

Getting people talking

When to tackle this section

This section is best tackled after you have discussed Section 3, *Christian conversations in our contemporary culture*. There are several important themes in the section and you may feel that not all of them can be addressed in a single session.

Methodist tradition

You may wish to start the conversation by asking people what has been most important to them about being a Methodist. If your group is ecumenical, of course people will want to share about the tradition to which they belong, or about belonging to a Local Ecumenical Partnership. In many cases, people will have had experience of belonging in more than one tradition. Make sure that you talk about distinctive emphases of other traditions if these are present in the group.

Taking it deeper

If you plan to address **question** (**3**) on p. 58 there are a number of ways in which you can extend the learning here. Reflecting on which hymns or songs people would choose for their funeral is potentially a very searching exercise, and they might wish to take this thought away with them for a week. Sharing the hymns, explaining why they were chosen and perhaps singing some of them or playing CD tracks will be both emotional and inspiring. It should be quite revealing as to what people hope their life of faith will have meant by the time they die.

The different Covenant Prayers

Discussion of the Covenant Prayer (opposite), in either version, can be challenging. Try to make sure that people feel safe to express which parts of the prayer they find themselves able to say, and which parts are really hard for them.

Modern version

I am no longer my own but yours.
Your will, not mine, be done in all things,
wherever you may place me,
in all that I do and in all that I may endure;
when there is work for me
and when there is none;
when I am troubled and when I am at peace.
Your will be done
when I am valued
and when I am disregarded;
when I find fulfilment
and when it is lacking;
when I have all things,
and when I have nothing.
I willingly offer
all I have and am to serve you,
as and where you choose.

Glorious and blessèd God,
Father, Son and Holy Spirit,
you are mine and I am yours.
May it be so for ever.
Let this covenant now made on earth
be fulfilled in heaven. Amen

Traditional version

I am no longer my own but yours.
Put me to what you will,
rank me with whom you will;
put me to doing,
put me to suffering;
let me be employed for you
or laid aside for you,
exalted for you
or brought low for you;
let me be full,
let me be empty,
let me have all things,
let me have nothing;
I freely and wholeheartedly yield all things
to your pleasure and disposal.

And now, glorious and blessèd God,
Father, Son and Holy Spirit,
you are mine and I am yours.
So be it.
And the covenant now made on earth,
let it be ratified in heaven. Amen

(taken from ***The Methodist Worship Book***, pp. 288-290)

Conversations with Methodist tradition

'Traditionally, Methodists have been expected to grow in the spiritual life. As such, Methodist membership is not an end point in itself, but is rather concerned with an ongoing growing in holiness, within a process of sanctification.'

Philip Drake, 'Joining the dots: Methodist membership and connectedness' in ***Unmasking Methodist Theology***, p. 134

'Jesus, confirm my heart's desire
To work, and speak, and think for thee;
Still let me guard the holy fire,
And still stir up thy gift in me.'

Charles Wesley, ***Hymns & Psalms*** 745, v. 3

The gift of grace enables Christian holiness or perfection

The image of the 'holy fire' captures quite well the concept of Christian holiness or perfection, which is Methodism's traditional way of speaking about growth in discipleship. Like the descent of the tongues of flame onto the heads of the earliest disciples at Pentecost, it is a pure gift of the Spirit. We 'catch fire' with the love of God. At the same time, keeping a fire continually burning requires ongoing vigilant work - watching for when more fuel needs adding, stirring the fire to ensure enough oxygen to keep the flames burning.

The tradition flowing from the story of the Wesleys has emphasised the assurance of the touch of God's Spirit on the heart - being 'strangely warmed' - a sense of truly feeling the reality of God's love as it is directly offered to all, whatever one's current state of sin. But putting into practice what it means to love God with one's whole heart, mind, soul and strength, was always thought of as also involving work and struggle. In John Wesley's teaching on 'perfect love', and in Methodist writings up to the 1950s, as Margaret Jones has shown, the constant themes are of 'love, growth, victory over sin, progress, new possibility, advance, transformation and the work of the Holy Spirit … The believer was expected to be filled with longing, to wrestle in prayer, participate in the other means of grace and to keep the rules of the Society to the utmost.' ('Growing in grace and holiness' in *Unmasking Methodist Theology,* pp. 155, 158-159)

The small group as the key place to nurture discipleship - the class meeting

When the Methodist 'societies' were founded, the practice very quickly grew up of dividing these societies into 'class meetings' of the membership. These small groups met weekly, and searching questions were posed as to the sins committed or the growth in holiness achieved that week. A rule of life involving personal conduct, prayer, Bible study and attendance at Holy Communion was expected. The rule of life also affected daily behaviour in the world of work - people were expected to 'do no harm' in their business and financial dealings, and to 'do good' through work on behalf of the needy. There is a sense that people were drawn to a movement that was serious about the practice of faith, and that there was a proactive desire to become a holier person, a more faithful follower of Jesus. The sense of being under judgement, and of

'A society is no other than a company of [persons] having the form and seeking the power of godliness, united in order to pray together, to receive the word of exhortation, and to watch over one another in love that they may help each other to work out their salvation.'

John Wesley, The rules of the united societies (*CPD*, volume 1, p. 73)

intention to change comes through strongly. Methodists were those who wanted to 'flee from the wrath to come'. They were 'seeking the power of godliness', willing to have others lovingly 'watch over' them (in the sense of holding them to account for the commitments they had made), in order that they might together 'work out' their salvation. Those who held responsibility or wanted to take things to a deeper level became part of the even more demanding 'bands.'

While there are places where class meetings still meet, in many parts of the Methodist Church the only remaining echo of such a strict practice is in fellowship groups or house groups. Many of these may meet for a variety of intentional conversations but it is very unlikely to be for the purpose of holding each other to account for the commitments of membership undertaken, indicated on the ticket of membership (as required in SO 631, *CPD* (2004)). Still less is it likely that people engage in public confession of sins committed over the week. Many might regard such a practice as psychologically unhealthy, and perhaps some of the historical class meetings were indeed driven by an authoritarian approach rather than being genuinely safe and open. In seeking to 'recover' Christian conversation, it is important that we find models which work in our contemporary culture, rather than simply reproduce old models.

Yet interestingly, there are places in our culture beyond the Church that have discovered the power of the intentionally accountable small group to effect and affirm desired change. The groups that are devoted to losing weight, or supporting recovering alcoholics or problem gamblers use very similar methods to those of the early class meetings. Strict challenge and loving peer support go hand in hand. Those who attend are encouraged and upheld by the positive goals of health and freedom that such groups espouse. But we no longer seem to want or expect such an ethos from our Church. Is this because our sense of what burdens us has altered? Or is that development in spirituality is now framed, not as the pursuit of greater holiness, but of finding more 'me-time'? Or is it because we no longer, on the whole, truly wish to change or think that we need to?

Questions for conversation:

1. What is your response to the questions asked in the previous paragraph?
2. Have you ever been a member of a supportive group which held you to account for the promises or choices you had made? What was the experience like? What can the Church learn from this?
3. Which are your three favourite hymns or songs? (A powerful way to focus your answer is to think about what you would want sung at your funeral.) What does your choice say about what lies at the heart of your Christian discipleship?

Do we still believe in the doctrine of sanctification?

The language of 'holiness', 'perfection' and 'sanctification' does not sit easily in modern parlance, and it is more than probable that many who attend Methodist churches now, and indeed many members, have not heard these terms expounded. Indeed the concept of 'perfection' is likely to be confused with a driven perfectionism, which many modern Methodists would eschew. The 'Methodical' approach to the Christian life may survive more vigorously in the popular mind than in reality (a 'Methodist upbringing' may still be thought of as rather strict, with implications of temperance and a strict Protestant work-ethic).

But there is potential for the Methodist approach to growth in discipleship to be reclaimed as a counter-cultural idea. The 'struggle' is not about an attempt to develop or improve oneself (as in self-help groups or therapies), but about the effort to surrender one's will to be at one with the loving will of God. This is about as far as it could be from the 'project of the self' mentioned earlier.

'The doctrine [of sanctification] remains with us in Charles Wesley's hymns, but the formative framework, and even, I suspect, the spiritual intention, have largely gone.'

Brian Beck, 'The elusive Methodist identity - who are we?'in ***The Epworth Review*** (2000, Volume 27, Number 4)

Questions for conversation:

1. What does the term 'Christian holiness' mean to you?
2. In what ways (if any) does it differ from the modern term 'spirituality'?

'Christ has many services to be done:
some are easy, others are difficult;
some bring honour, others bring
reproach;
some are suitable to our natural
inclinations and material interests,
others are contrary to both.'

from the Covenant Service in
The Methodist Worship Book, p. 288.

The call to a covenant relationship

The Covenant Service is acknowledged to be one of the jewels in the Methodist liturgical crown that it brings to the ecumenical table. The 2003 enthronement service for the Archbishop of Canterbury used it at a solemn moment of the liturgy. It was adapted from earlier traditions and introduced into Methodist worship by John Wesley as a means of regularly reaffirming our commitment as disciples and followers of Jesus. Yet it is now felt by many to be too difficult and too intense.

The service, which is full of the assurance of God's love for us, in whose power alone we are able to undertake such promises, includes a profound meditation on how we can discern what is being asked of us. It is clear that the 'many services' Christ may ask of us go well beyond the realm of Church responsibilities, and could involve social reproach or financial hardship. But there is a beautiful balance, which suggests the possibility that our calling will include undertaking activities that we enjoy and that will bring us prosperity and honour. It is impossible to rule out hardship, but neither is the hair-shirt approach at all reliable in determining what God wants of us. It is about genuinely offering ourselves – 'no longer our own but yours'. It is the giving up of our own agency and right to choose which is so hard.

The older version of the Covenant Prayer has been criticised in recent years. People in particular have resisted the phrase 'put me to suffering', as if God deliberately willed us to experience pain. However the word simply means the opposite of 'doing'; it is the state of waiting or passivity, of 'being done to' in some way, and parallels the next phrase, being 'employed' or 'laid aside'. The desire for control, agency and choice is a very strongly encouraged stance in our society, and it is not surprising that we resist truly offering God our willingness to let both agency and passivity be 'for you'. However, to believe that God cannot be served except in active 'doing' will lead us to marginalise those whose calling is now to lay things down, or who do indeed have to endure suffering in the modern sense. The revised version of the prayer clarifies the point by referring to 'all that I do, and in all that I may endure'.

'Put me to doing,
put me to suffering;
let me be employed for you
or laid aside for you.'

from the Covenant Service in *The Methodist Worship Book*, p. 290.

Questions for conversation:

1. Look at the two versions of the Covenant Prayer in *The Methodist Worship Book* (pages 288-290) and reproduced on page 55. What are the key differences between them? Which version do you prefer, and why?
2. What do you value most about the Covenant Service as a whole? Which aspects of it do you find most challenging?

'The Gospel of Christ knows no religion but social; no holiness but social holiness.'

John Wesley, ***A Plain Account of Christian Perfection***

'A Christian is called by God to trust and follow Jesus Christ; to keep company with him; to learn from his words and actions; and to share in his mission, in the power of the Holy Spirit, in company with other Christians.'

A Catechism for the use of the people called Methodists, p. 4

Social holiness

The phrase 'social holiness' has had a continuing appeal for Methodists even where enthusiasm for the exploration of personal holiness has waned, possibly because it has echoes of the term 'social gospel'. It is true that an emphasis on social justice and caring within the community has been a continuing emphasis for Methodists. But what Wesley was referring to was the opposite of individualism. The calling of a Christian disciple can only be lived, as the *Catechism* makes clear, 'in company with other Christians'. Methodist membership must be registered in an actual local church situation, among a particular group of flawed and hopeful fellow disciples.

This concept is in marked contrast with the prevailing cultural enthusiasms for 'spirituality', which are marketed to the individual to pursue and customise to fit his or her own private path to wholeness. However it is important that the individual who is trying to explore honestly what they believe and where they can find meaning in life actually finds a group of Christians where 'company' means something. This is to be the place where the disciple can explore what it means to 'keep company' with God; so it is not enough to offer a fellowship which is routine, sociable and undemanding - and which may suit some ages and temperaments much better than it does others.

Indeed, if the Christian company on offer is made up only of people who are socially similar to ourselves, the alarm bells should ring. The older Covenant Prayer shows awareness of our tendency to congregate with those most like ourselves, and asks that we put the choice of our company, congenial or not, into God's hands: 'rank me with whom you will'. We need to be prepared for the surprises on offer at God's great feast. We are stretched sometimes in making and sustaining relationships with people we don't always understand - it stretches us in grace.

The requirement for Methodists to discern our calling in company with others is at the heart of *connexion*, which finds its most notable ecclesiological expression in the Conference. We need to 'confer' in order to know where God is calling us now; we need to meet, to 'see each other's face'.

'Rank me with whom you will'

Covenant Service,
The Methodist Worship Book, p. 290

'And are we yet alive,
And see each other's face?'

Charles Wesley, ***Hymns & Psalms*** 707 v. 1,
sung to open the Conference

Questions for conversation:

1. Over the course of your Christian life, which group or 'company' of Christians has had the most influence on you? Why?
2. Who do you share deeply with today? Who might you ask to join you in sharing deeply about faith?

'Many long for God, yet are prevented from finding him.'

Current blocks to conversation within the Church

Getting people talking

When to tackle this section

You may find it helpful to tackle this section along with Section 2, *Talking about our faith*. Because the focus here is on problems, it is probably best not to address them without having first discussed positive questions such as the meaning of our discipleship. It will be important for the group to trust each other enough to be frank about the local ethos without the session turning into a general moan about all that is wrong with the Church.

Achieving a constructive outcome

It is important to express the aims of the session in constructive terms, as a good conversation in this area will ideally lead to some energy for creating actual plans to improve things. Explain that the point of considering 'blocks' is not to attribute blame, but to free people up to mention matters that are important, but may previously have been hard to raise. This means that you should aim:

- to identify which are the most recognisable 'blocks' in your context (the issues mentioned here or others), and to focus on these;
- to give time to **question (3)** and explore actions that could be taken to overcome these blocks. It may be helpful to ask people to buzz in twos or threes, saying in positive terms how they would like it to be if a particular block had been resolved.

Considering people's feelings

This session is potentially sensitive, because your group may well include people who may see themselves as at least partly responsible for a church ethos where blocks to Christian conversation exist. Remind people about the paragraphs on p. 18 about the *Methodist Church Life Profile*, which gives a connexion-wide picture – the ethos is much more pervasive than a single local church or circuit. Changing a culture or an ethos is notoriously difficult.

Be aware that people may be quite defensive at this point in the conversation, and always seek to take blame away from any individual, while staying firm about the desirability of enabling people to speak freely about faith.

What are the current blocks to conversation within the Church?

The exercise of seeking God and learning how to love and serve God in our lives is deeply attractive, but also perhaps quite frightening. So it is that the Church, which exists to support that search, that love and that service, somehow manages to frustrate its own ends by providing a culture where conversation around this most important of topics is effectively, if unconsciously, blocked in a variety of ways.

'Many long for God, yet are prevented from finding him.'

Mark Davis, ***Walking on the Shore***, p. 80

'The primary focus of discipleship is the service of God and his mission in the world. In this it differs from ministry, with its key focus of nurture, development and leadership of the Church. The tendency in our Church culture is to see ministry as a normative category for discipleship. This often leads to a Church-oriented approach to discipleship.'

Education for Discipleship draft report of the Hind working group

Identifying taking a church role with being a disciple

Too often it is assumed that those who are serious about their discipleship will express that by taking on a responsible role within the church. The *Methodist Church Life Profile* (see page 18) revealed that only one in four Methodist respondents did not have a particular church role. Consequently, the conversations we expect to prioritise in church may tend to focus around church business. We may be formally commissioned for work undertaken in church - but get very little support for the work or conversation about the issues that we face in our everyday life in which the majority of our discipleship must be worked out. This creates

'I spend an hour a week teaching Sunday School and they haul me up to the front of the church to pray for me. The rest of the week I'm a full-time teacher and the church has never prayed for me. That says it all.'

Teacher quoted in Mark Greene, ***Supporting Christians at work***, p.5

'The majority of church members have no idea of the kind of things I do in my professional life, the decisions I make (decisions that often affect people's jobs and lives), or the pressures of a modern business.'

Methodist in his thirties quoted in ***Methodism and the Future***, p. 87

the impression that the place of significant discipleship, vocation and ministry is the church culture only, and that those who do not have time to commit here are not serving God properly. This impression silences Christians about their work in the world, and leaves them unsupported by the kinds of conversation that could help them understand their context of discipleship.

Church 'business' that crowds out all other types of conversation

It would seem obvious that the worship of God and the opportunity to deepen our understanding of what it means to be disciples together are the primary motives for gathering as Church. Even the central business meeting of the local church, the Church Council, is supposed to start with 'Conversation on the work of God' (*CPD* (2004), p. 763). However, local church meetings can be very business-led, and when people have committed themselves to a punishing schedule of church business meetings, there is sometimes very little other time to engage explicitly in the ongoing exploration of faith. Perhaps because of this, and because some people want to meet their socialising needs also through attendance at meetings, business meetings themselves can become lengthy, rambling and ultimately indecisive. Meetings like this are hardly likely to attract younger adults, who are accustomed to a pressured work culture and whose available time is very precious, especially when they have young children.

Socialising that in fact only welcomes a limited range of people

This is a tricky one, because it seems to be the case that people want to 'belong' before they grow into belief. So in a way there must be an attraction to a group with which it is possible to identify. Many people in the oldest generation of the church have grown up and grown old with a peer group of friends. Younger people often find it hard to settle into a church community because of the lack of peers with whom to connect. Often a 'critical mass' of younger adults has to be reached before such people are retained. But Jesus' warnings about the dangers of identifying socialising with the kingdom need to be heeded. Church people who are mostly social friends may unawarely exclude those who are not their type - and they may be disinclined to be challenging to each other in talking about things that go beneath the surface of ordinary social norms.

The obligation to be 'nice'

One of the problems with adopting a purely sociable model for conversing with each other is that we will overemphasise niceness and harmony and confuse these with Christian love. If we have no ways of challenging each other

'The last thing I want to do after a day of meetings is to spend a further two-and-a-half hours in a meeting where the majority of agenda items should be delegated ... [This is] the point, it seems to me, when matters of faith and theology are so important: providing guidance on how to prioritise.'

Methodist in his thirties quoted in ***Methodism and the Future***, p. 87

'"Fellowship" can too easily become a theological slogan covering up the private, cosy socialising of an exclusive group. The party may actually not be open to very many people.'

Clive Marsh, 'A training ground for forgiveness: Methodism and "Fellowship"' in ***Methodism and the Future***, p. 108

'Old people, although I can talk to them, seem to think they're always right. I hate arguing with old people 'cos I have to respect them - they're going to be more insulted if I disagreed than I would be if they disagreed.'

Young person asked to comment on blocks to conversation

and registering disagreement in the pursuit of truth, certain people will be silenced and certain insights, which might have benefited everybody, will be left unexplored. However, negative thoughts will probably emerge anyway elsewhere, through gossip and backbiting. There is a huge value in different generations listening to each other, but conversational norms may differ and there needs to be conscious mutual respect and agreement about ground rules.

In small churches, especially those in settled communities, it can be the case that those who come to church are indeed each other's socialising group as well. There may be blood, marriage, or long-standing social ties between a high proportion of the congregation. As one member of a rural congregation said to a new minister who had not served in a rural context before, 'If you kick one of us, we all limp.' There can also be long-standing grudges or family feuds. These realities may make speaking openly problematic.

Avoiding difficult subjects

It can be a strange experience, when the news is full of issues or events that divide people (including Christians), to come to church and find that there is no mention of such subjects in the sermon. It can be like existing in two different thought worlds. Some may find this a welcome relief. Most would find it irritating if the preacher raised a controversial subject but showed no awareness that other Christians could take a different line from themselves. But the majority would feel more able to raise the subject in conversation over coffee with each other, if the preacher had addressed the range of views and tried to wrestle with scripture in the light of events in the world.

There is another class of 'difficult subject' which may well be avoided, in addition to those that may be politically controversial, and these include such painful matters as facing one's own death. A minister reports that she regularly addresses the matter of death with older women's meetings, and receives in feedback a huge sense of relief and gratitude. It is on the minds of the members of the meeting, but previously there has been no cultural permission given to bring up such things.

A third kind of 'difficult subject' concerns the Church itself. Many people have felt hurt by the Church (whether the Methodist Church or another), and this damage may be blocking their way to God. If there is to be reconciliation, it will be necessary to talk about matters which it may be painful to hear about. We need to give permission for these conversations to happen.

'"Dodgy" subjects are often avoided in the pulpit. Lack of education from the pulpit often makes us less comfortable with discussing in a church context. People avoid offence!'

Young person asked to comment on blocks to conversation

'I read out to my pastoral visitors the bits from Standing Orders that entail talking with people about fulfilling the commitments of membership, and they were frankly horrified.'

A minister

'On the few occasions I've raised some of my theological doubts with a minister, they've told me it doesn't really matter as long as I believe in God, and then just prayed with me, which has been nice and helpful, but it doesn't help me address the bigger questions.'

Young adult asked to comment on the theme of this report

Not expecting faith to be discussed

We have moved so far from the culture where people attended weekly class meetings and in those meetings were invited to examine their hearts, that class leaders and pastoral visitors are usually not even asked to tackle conversations about faith at all. A recent pack devised for pastoral visitors covers a range of updated approaches to the pastoral conversation, but the only hint of 'spiritual' conversation is a suggestion about offering to pray with those they visit. Those who prepared the pack were conscious of how delicate the matter is. They were aware that, in spite of what SO 631 (*CPD* (2004)) declares about the duties of class leaders and pastoral visitors, many pastoral visitors feel ill-equipped and unsuited to spiritual conversation and embarrassed by the thought of praying with those they visit. They conceive of their work in social or befriending terms. However, there are some who do engage in spiritual conversation in skilled and sensitive ways.

There is a danger, in the context of church life, of making the implicit assumption that it is not *necessary* to have a whole range of conversations. It is as if we believe that, if you are in church at all, you are sort 'paid-up' to certain beliefs. All-important conversations are then effectively bypassed.

Fellowship groups that have no clear purpose, but never die

It is a common complaint of house groups that they all already know each other's views on a range of subjects, or that they do not know what to talk about. The cry is always for suitable material to discuss. There may be a sense of boredom, and members may gradually vote with their feet. But there is a sense that to end the group formally would represent a failure. Meanwhile no other initiative can start instead, as the 'loyal' group members have to keep showing up. Groups however do have a natural life and need to review regularly their purpose for existing - otherwise they do slip into a habit of relating, which is more social than anything else. That is why it is hard to ask the 'rude' question about why on earth we go on meeting.

Fellowship groups where it isn't safe to disagree

Although groups will be much more productive if they have a clear purpose in meeting, and the boundaries of that purpose are kept, it is important that this clarity does not become a straitjacket. In a true conversation, all parties to it must be open to being transformed by the process. Safety in a group needs to include safety to disagree with the leader or those who express their views most strongly. Assumptions need to be checked out, differences debated with respect, and confidentiality honoured.

'Busy commuter-belt professionals will give hours to something that delivers, but resent every second spent in an anodyne, flaky group.'

Mark Greene, 'Learning to live, living to learn' in ***Imagine***, p. 23

'What's "nurture"?... It's forcing something to grow the way you want it to.'

from a discussion among teenagers about the theme of this report

'Fellowship is about openness … rather than … a context within which answers to questions are assumed, party lines must be adopted and people's actual issues, questions, doubts and affirmations are not taken seriously.'

Clive Marsh, 'A training ground for forgiveness: Methodism and "Fellowship"' in ***Methodism and the Future***, p. 102

'Christians experience growth and transition in their spiritual life just as in their physical and emotional lives. While this growth is always a work of grace, it does not occur uniformly. Spiritual growth in Christ is a dynamic process marked by awakening, birth, growth and maturation.'

The Book of Discipline of the United Methodist Church, para. 133

Failing to 'differentiate'

There is a need for age-appropriate discipleship reflecting both the individual's spiritual age and their actual age. Research suggests that the Church's historic approach to the discipleship of children and young people has been flawed. Equipping a child for a life of discipleship is more than telling her what it is believed by adults that she needs to know. The heavily didactic approach they experienced when children has left many adults very ill-prepared to cope with the questions and challenges of a life of faith. Children and young people need to be enabled to become thinking and mature disciples. Similarly young adults, those in their middle years, the recently retired and the elderly should be allowed to grow and explore their discipleship in the face of changing life patterns and circumstances.

While there is some recognition that people feel more able to converse at depth with people their own age (youth fellowships), or who are at a similar life-stage (parent and toddler clubs), less attention may be given to considering the stages of Christian maturity in discipleship. Many churches may focus on the 'entry point' stage (*Alpha* courses), but there is often less attention to the various needs of mature disciples, who need challenging to grow in ways that go beyond just being given lots of responsibility for church business.

Ministers who make a point of visiting potential church members report that they often hear people say, 'I've been attending for years and no-one has ever asked me about membership before'. People who have been members for a long time may never have been presented with encouragement to make their growth in discipleship a matter of accountability. There is not much thinking around, concerning the demands of discipleship in later life. So it can be that stalwarts of the church have been inducted into a concept of discipleship that is identified as being willing to run the church, and they have nobly continued to do just that, well beyond their retirement. They may be feeling 'put upon' and space for them to explore a different path of discipleship may be lacking, and younger adults may feel less than enthusiastic about volunteering for tasks that are firmly in the hands of the oldest generation or are done in an old-fashioned way.

Questions for conversation on the whole section:

1. Which of the 'blocks' to conversation described above ring any bells in your church?
2. Are there other blocks that you can identify?
3. What actions to overcome these blocks can you think of?

A restored conversation

'We have a wonderful
sense of sharing in the
inexpressible mystery of
God and the inexplicable
hope that is in us.'

Getting people talking

When to tackle this session

This session should be tackled after you have discussed the other parts of this resource that you intend to address. Taken along with the contents of Appendices A and B, which provides a wide range of structured initiatives and ideas for churches to try, the intention should be to agree where your conversation has taken you and to make sure that there are practical plans for following up your insights.

Practical plans

- Review the 'practical implications' you have noted after any of the sections, especially your discussion of Section 6, *Current blocks to conversation within the Church.*
- Ask a group member or two to look through Appendices A and B beforehand, and come with suggestions about what could work effectively in your church, to encourage intentional Christian conversation. Allow plenty of discussion on these ideas or others and choose which to pursue.
- Identify the first steps that need to be taken and agree who will take them.
- Let us know your plans! (See contact details on page 6)

Reviewing the life of the group

You could start the session by reading out Clive Scott's version of the first chapter of John's Gospel, see page 81.

Ending the group

Do not be tempted to carry the group on, if your contract was for a limited series of meetings. If there is enthusiasm for a continuing conversation group, ask someone to set up a new group, with a new remit.

A restored conversation

These are the assumptions made by the working group, about the kind of Christian conversation we are seeking to recover.

- It will take **time**: it requires us to slow down, to get to know each other better. Clive Marsh writes of 'the relatively little time which we often assume we need, to experience fellowship with other people' ('A training ground for forgiveness: Methodism and "fellowship"' in *Methodism and the Future,* p. 109).
- The conversation with each other needs to be rooted in our conversation with God. In both conversations, we need to build up **trust in the relationship**.
- The conversation needs all parties in it to be **open to transformation**. We should not assume that someone knows exactly where the conversation is going to end up.
- It will be purposive and **intentional**. This needs to be explicit, otherwise the socialising norms about the level of conversation will take over.
- For those who have taken the step of becoming a church member, there needs to be a place where we are asked to be **accountable** for our growth in discipleship. This is as true for ministers as for lay people.

'An older woman in my church often talks with me about her life story and attests to the faith which has sustained her through many tragedies. She never articulates any theological theories, but expresses the unanswerable questions she lives with (along the lines of why do bad things happen to good people). A lot of the communication is non-verbal. We have a wonderful sense of sharing the inexpressible mystery of God and the inexplicable hope that is in us.'

Viv Morrissey, Training and Development Officer

The conversation we are speaking about, then, is one in which:

- we meditate on the things of God in the light of our own experience, and become able to talk safely and freely, to take pleasure in the exploration as we find words and share silence;
- we examine ourselves and consider how our lives, choices, activities, relationships and patterns of consumption do or don't reflect the life of God;
- we are able to identify, share and celebrate God's action in our lives;
- we joyfully encourage each other together to follow in the way of Christ and to grow and learn;
- we recognise the different ways people learn and are able to express themselves;
- we identify what resources we need to take further the exploration of our faith.

Of course, if we do re-learn to talk to each other about what matters most, we shall find ultimately that words are not enough.

In 1516, Erasmus produced his own translation of the New Testament, in which he translated 'logos' from the prologue of John's Gospel not as 'Word' but 'Conversation'.

John 1:1-14 revisited

It all arose out of a conversation, conversation within God, in fact the conversation was God. So God started the discussion, and everything came out of this, and nothing happened without consultation.

This was the life, life that was the light of men, shining in the darkness, a darkness which neither understood nor quenched its creativity.

John, a man sent by God, came to remind people about the nature of the light so that they would observe. He was not the subject under discussion, but the bearer of an invitation to join in.

The subject of the conversation, the original light, came into the world, the world that had arisen out of his willingness to converse. He fleshed out the words but the world did not understand. He came to those who knew the language, but they did not respond. Those who did became a new creation (his children). They read the signs and responded.

These children were born out of sharing in the creative activity of God. They heard the conversation still going on, here, now, and took part, discovering a new way of being people.

To be invited to share in a conversation about the nature of life was for them, a glorious opportunity not to be missed.

* In the second paragraph, the Greek term translated here as 'light of men' is inclusive of all humanity.

Questions for conversation:

1 What do we mean by discipleship?

Now is a good time to re-visit the understandings of discipleship that you shared earlier on in Section 1. Look again at pictures they drew or definitions they agreed.

- Has your understanding of your discipleship changed in any way?

(Allow people to work individually and then share.)

2 What kind of conversation have we experienced?

Using the material on pp. 79-80:

- How far have these qualities of Christian conversation in fact been part of our experience in this group?
- What have we each particularly valued in what we have received from each other during this time?

Appendices

'There is room for lots of creativity and for trying a variety of ways of shifting the culture.'

Structured initiatives for enabling intentional and transformative conversation

All that we know about the dynamics of human groups of various sizes suggests that it is in the small group (no more than 12 people) that a powerful intimacy becomes possible. At this size, there is the potential for individuals to feel safe to talk at a personal level. Larger groups inevitably become more formal in their interactions and many people will not speak at all in that context. This means that some version of the small group is the natural place to foster transformative conversation.

However, convening a small group is not a magic solution. Without conscious leadership, a clear agreed intention, some sort of agreed structure and regular reflection on process, small groups will tend to display a range of unconscious behaviours that undermine the reason why the group was set up. It is very possible for a group to become an unwelcoming clique, for it to collude in avoiding the task it has officially agreed to do, for it to be sabotaged or dominated by difficult individuals, and so on. And, as we have seen above, groups that are not deliberately limited in their lifespan do in any case begin to stagnate naturally. It is hard to name these dynamics, because people who have derived huge benefit from each other's support almost always want to go on meeting.

Churches have tried a number of more intentional approaches to the small group as a place to foster discipleship. It is clear from the popularity of the *Alpha* course that people do welcome the opportunity to talk about the meaning of life at depth, especially in a context where questions are welcomed and the whole atmosphere (ie: meeting around a meal) is designed to enable conversation. There is a combination of sociability and hospitality, along with an intentional structure for the conversations. One of the features of *Alpha* has been its attraction for those who have already been worshipping and practising as Christians for some time. This may indicate that they were never offered the chance to enter into important conversations at the point where they joined the church's fellowship.

Recovering Christian conversation

Mark Davis developed, over ten years, a project that was originally known as *Time + Space.* As a Catholic R.E. teacher, Davis was first drawn to explore how to create groups in which it was safe to explore faith at depth by encountering the questions raised by the parents of his pupils. They had received some Church teaching but had got stuck at a preliminary stage while not really having a context to explore their own experience of God.

His book *Walking on the Shore* explores how we have lost the art of spiritual conversation and proposes a method for recovering it. It is important for the approach that the group leader is trained in facilitation. This includes an understanding of the principles of how small groups operate and what sort of attitudes are needed in order to create the 'unconditional positive regard' that can allow people to speak without fear of judgement about what is of the deepest importance to them. A faith-sharing meeting using his approach would consist of an agreed number of sessions, with a commitment to attend and a membership that does not change for the agreed but limited period. A typical structure would be:

- preparation (prayer and preparation of the room space);
- welcome, silence and prayer;
- a prepared stimulus for reflection and period of individual reflection;
- sharing of insight and conversation;
- review and closing prayers responding to the insights of the session;
- refreshments and informal chat.

Disciple

Disciple is a 34-week journey through 70% of the Bible. It combines personal study of the scriptures with a weekly group meeting of those who have studied the same passages. It is not for the fainthearted, requiring about half an hour of study a day and a two and a half hour meeting each week, but those who have experienced it talk of it being a life-changing experience, which gives them confidence to talk about their faith and helps them to discover their gifts. The course begins where people are, and invites them to bring their questions and reflect on the scriptures in the light of their experience. It exposes group members to the best of mainstream biblical scholarship across a wide spectrum of theological starting points through both written material and video clips. Churches and circuits that undertake the course usually find that in time people's gifts are released for mission and ministry, and that people serve with much more understanding of what it means to be a disciple of Jesus. There are follow-up courses: *Disciple 2* concentrates on Genesis, Exodus, Luke and Acts and helps people to go deeper by practising some spiritual disciplines each week; *Disciple 3* concentrates on the prophets and the letters, explaining what it means to be a Christian community.

Further details are available from mph, 4 John Wesley Road, Werrington, Peterborough PE4 6ZP (tel: 01733 325002) (website: www.mph.org.uk).

Cell Church

Cell Church is a movement which focuses on the small group as *being an expression of Church* rather than being a peripheral and optional extra. It is a value-based way of being Church, with six key values:

- **Jesus at the centre;**
- **the Church as a community of openness, honesty and sacrificial love;**
- **every member growing;**
- **every member in ministry;**
- **every member a witness;**
- **healthy cells multiply.**

Cells are not meetings, but communities which meet. Cell meetings vary in shape and frequency, but the most common practice is to use the four 'W's: welcome, worship, word and witness. The ice-breaker used in the welcome is important in order to set the level of the meeting, to ensure that people learn new things about each other and to ensure that newcomers are on an equal footing with others. There are no set patterns of worship but the emphasis is on participation and the result can be very innovative. The 'word' section addresses how the living word revealed in scripture applies to our lives, and 'witness' is about relational evangelism and social outreach. Because cells are communities and a sharing of lives (and not meetings), they also meet in other ways and at other times, apart from the 'formal' cell meeting.

A cell starts small (5-8) to allow for growth, but should not normally get larger than 14, when it multiplies into two groups of 7. The principle of multiplication is vital. This ensures that the group does not stagnate but keeps growing and looking outwards. To enable growth, cell leaders need to be people who encourage the development of the gifts of cell participants, and who in particular can 'apprentice' a new leader. In a church which completely adopts the cell church principle, the congregation is a gathering of the cells.

Details about the Methodist Cell Church Network are available from Revd Peter Pillinger, 59 Albion Crescent, Lincoln LN1 1EB (e-mail: rev@pillinger.net).

Covenant Discipleship

Covenant Discipleship groups are small groups of people who want to grow in their relationship with Jesus Christ through mutual accountability and support. They meet once a week for an hour to pray and 'watch over one another in love'. Each group writes its own covenant, based on Jesus' greatest commandments (Matthew 22:36-40). This covenant then guides their discipleship and serves as the agenda for the weekly meeting.

The shape of the weekly meeting is like a 'compass heading' for discipleship that keeps group members on course in their walk with Christ. The format is to begin with prayer and then to go through the covenant, clause by clause, with the leader asking every member in turn, including himself/herself, to give an account of his/her discipleship during the past week in light of the covenant. The meeting is not to exceed one hour. This requires a brisk pace and a focus on the agenda of the covenant. However, as the group develops the skill of mutual accountability, sharing increasingly takes place in an atmosphere of trust and Christian fellowship. The meeting is not where discipleship happens. It is where we *make sure* it happens.

At the moment there are only a few groups meeting in the U.K.. More groups are sought to help pilot the project.

Further details are available from Revd Jenny Impey, Priesthaus, East Road, Maidenhead SL6 1PH (e-mail: jennyimpey@aol.com).

Somewhere Else

Another entry point to discipleship may grow organically out of an engagement with personal story and identity. An emerging church in Liverpool City Centre works with this process gathering a community around the baking and sharing of bread. *Somewhere Else* is the name given to this gathering, which has engaged with many excluded by conventional church structures as well as committed Christians looking for a different space to explore new ideas. The intention of *Somewhere Else* is to provide a place of inclusivity and safety where all can remember their personal stories and find some quiet in the day. Out of this process a community has emerged in which the gospel story is heard and prayers said. Through the simple task of bread-making many have grown in their depth of faith and a number have chosen to be baptised. This is an intentional community rather than a church plant. The bread-making has facilitated the faith journey of many, giving a holistic approach to discipleship.

For more information see Barbara Glasson's I am Somewhere Else – a gospel reflection from an emerging church *(Darton Longman and Todd, October 2005) or contact Somewhere Else, Second floor, 96 Bold Street, Liverpool L1 4HY.*

Godly Play

Godly Play is a programme that has been developed by Jerome Berryman, an Episcopal priest in the United States, which is increasingly finding a warm reception among churches here. Its purpose is 'to teach children the art of using religious language - parables, sacred stories, silence and liturgical action - to help them become more fully aware of the mystery of God's presence in their lives' (www.godlyplay.org).

Based on the Montessori way of teaching, Godly Play shows how children (and adults) can experience God in the midst of play, through retelling Bible stories with the use of simple visual aids, encouraging the use of the imagination. As the story is told, the listeners are drawn into what is going on through a series of open-ended questions, so that they are not simply passive, but become participants in the meaning. When the story has been told, participants have the chance to explore feelings and insights through painting, drawing or modelling with clay or plasticine. Teachers and children learn together, in a church setting and within a clearly defined faith community. Some adults who have experienced Godly Play bear witness that the meaning of a particular familiar story has come alive for them for the first time.

For further details about Godly Play, contact Revd Keith Underhill, 7 Hastings Avenue, Ilford IG6 1DZ (e-mail:thoseatnumber7@aol.com).

Ideas for churches to try, that could shift the culture about conversation

In addition to structured small groups or wholly experimental church contexts, there is room for lots of creativity and for trying a variety of ways of shifting the culture in the direction of deepening the conversations that happen. Some of these could be gentle, small steps towards encouraging new ways of conversing. Others will require more planning, agreement and effort.

Freeing up ministers, deacons and lay workers for more in depth conversations

For example, one minister has introduced a practice of doing something quite different in church life during Lent. Having cancelled all other meetings, she asked members of her congregations to invite her to come and celebrate Holy Communion in their home – not as an emergency situation for the housebound, but in order to experience the Eucharist in the place where they normally ate, using their own bread and wine. People were free to invite in whom they chose, including family members or neighbours. In the event, people placed themselves in relation to the table in a variety of ways: they went out of the house, they stayed in the room but watched from a distance, they came and joined in. The conversations arising from the experiences have still not stopped! Interestingly, it was not the most faithful pillars of the local church that were the most receptive to the idea.

Taking a 'sabbatical' from church meetings

This would be for an agreed period, to free up people to be involved in some different conversations. The pressures of modern church life make it difficult to find time to re-evaluate how we talk to each other. The working group proposes that churches might undertake a supported 'sabbatical'. During this time, churches could continue conducting worship, prayer meetings, children's and young people's work, fruitful community-based outreach and *necessary* committees, but have a break from all other meetings and groups.

During the sabbatical an invitation could be extended to everyone within the church to have a conversation with their minister or other appropriate person to talk about their discipleship, gifts and their personal growth.

The Newbury and Hungerford Circuit planned just such an experimental period during 2005, and organised a wide variety of opportunities for people to refresh their faith and discipleship, while church business meetings were suspended between the new year and Easter. Planning for this 'sabbatical' took effort and time, but it would be valuable to know how people responded to the exercise.

Timetabling church business meetings

One church has business meetings only on alternate weeks, so that there are always weeks throughout the year for 'non-meeting' activities.

Encouraging testimony

This can be done in a variety of ways. Personal testimony from a range of people (not just the minister or the preacher) can be very powerful in opening up conversation, even when the person giving testimony is not very articulate.

Here are some ideas:

- Members of the congregation who come from or are familiar with other parts of the World Church may be invited to share different traditions and practices. For instance, it is normal in Jamaican churches to include a time when people can share how God has been active in their lives during the week. Those who come to live here notice things about British culture which we may fail to see. Liberian Methodist pastor Akoi Bazzie, commenting on the difference between church life in Sheffield and in the refugee camp in Guinea where he had spent years of his life, said, 'We are not used to being so quiet about what God has done for us.' (*Methodist Recorder*, 23 December 2004)
- One church regularly gives over part of the 'sermon slot' in worship during Lent to members of the congregation who have been asked to tell their story of faith - how they come to be worshipping in this church here and now. Often moving, these stories give rise to important conversations over coffee afterwards.

- An *agape* or 'love feast' could be held, in which a shared, relaxed meal is begun with prayer and interspersed with songs. Invite some individuals to prepare beforehand a testimony on a given theme. You will probably find that, after the prepared testimonies have been given, others will volunteer to tell the story of how God has led and supported them.
- *The Methodist Worship Book* offers opportunities to invite testimonies to encourage each other. These include Holy Communion for Ordinary Seasons (Third Service) and for Pentecost; the service of Confirmation and Reception into Membership; the Celebration of Christian Renewal.
- If giving explicitly personal testimony feels difficult, many people are able to choose a favourite hymn and explain what it means to them. Churches could hold a *Songs of Praise* event and ask people to say why they want a certain hymn.

Encouraging people to make links between working life and faith

The impression that only 'churchy' roles (or perhaps certain caring professions such as doctors and nurses) are really vocational in Christian terms is so strong in some church circles that positive permission and encouragement may need to be given to talk about other work dilemmas or areas of effective ministry.

- Make sure that a range of professions is regularly prayed for by asking people with different jobs to lead intercessions, focusing on their needs for prayer.
- Try setting up a fellowship or Bible study group where the point is for people to share what it means to be a faithful Christian disciple in their work context.
- Occasionally invite speakers from different professions to address this question from their perspective from the pulpit.
- When you invite testimony, make it clear that you want to hear about 'ordinary' experience as well as 'religious' experience, so that people are encouraged by the stories of God at work in the world and start to make similar connections with their own experience.

In addition, churches could try the following:

- Exploring with pastoral visitors and class leaders what is their practice and find ways to enable sharing about how to have conversation at depth. 'Active listening' is something that most people can learn to do, and can draw forth different levels of conversation beyond the purely sociable.

- Creating film or book clubs that offer ways in to talking about issues of deep significance to contemporary life. Sometimes it is easier to talk about what matters by focusing on a fictional story.
- Asking people what they need and want in terms of in-depth conversation - this may relate to their age, life-stage or stage of Christian maturity. Why not have a 'suggestion box' in church for the guidance of preachers, where people can anonymously post questions they want to explore?
- Instituting the occasional 'heckle the preacher' service, where a brief sermon is followed by a more conversational session with a roving microphone. One church runs a monthly 'Talk Back' session after the service. Those who wish to can stay for half an hour and raise questions with the preacher about the sermon. The session is facilitated by a Church Steward.
- Inviting house groups to review what is their purpose in meeting, and perhaps to dissolve to let a new thing happen. Or deliberately organising groups that are time-limited, so that their focus and purpose does not 'drift'.
- Exploring some alternative ways of listening to children and young people and encouraging them in intentional Christian conversation. For instance, Godly Play could be introduced, or imaginative ways of soliciting children's and young people's questions about God and faith. Various episodes of *The Simpsons* have been found productive in this respect.
- Offering some easy entry points to conversation, eg: different sorts of worship gathering such as coffee clubs where conversation is part of the event.
- Offering some more demanding options as well, where people are expecting to help each other explore how to be a disciple in the world.

Questions for conversation on the whole section:

1. Among all the initiatives and suggestions outlined above, which strike you as ideas that could work in your church? What ideas of your own occur to you?
2. What would be the first steps to take in encouraging your church to explore these ideas seriously?

Resources

Mark Davis, *Walking on the Shore – a way of sharing faith in groups* (Chelmsford, Matthew James Publishing Limited, 2002)

See section above on *Recovering Christian conversation* (page 85). The book is a beautifully-designed exploration of Mark Davis' methods for small faith-sharing groups, and the experience of reading it is much more than an information gathering exercise - it is like going on a retreat. The reader will find that the gentle but probing questions lead into a wealth of personal insight and deeper prayer.

Brenda Woods, *Come as you are* (Peterborough, mph, 2004)

This is a ten-session course exploring Christian discipleship and membership in the Methodist Church. The material covers basic Christian doctrine and the history, structure and mission of the Methodist Church. Each session is designed to last two hours and to be led by one or two facilitators. The material is structured to allow individual reflection, work in pairs and whole group discussion (maximum ten people). One session focuses on the life of discipleship with particular reference to Methodist membership. The course is based primarily on biblical material but also draws on illustrations from art, music and poetry. Participants need to be reasonably literate and the illustrations may not be accessible in all contexts. The material is well-presented and is written to be used both with those new to faith and those wishing to go on a 'refresher' course.

Presence - a workbook to help promote and sustain an effective Christian presence in villages (Peterborough, mph, 2004)

A large proportion of Methodist chapels are small and rural. This workbook is aimed at those who live and worship in the countryside, and was inspired by the resolution at Conference 2001 which expressed Methodism's solemn commitment to rural communities. There is a thought-provoking essay by David Emison which questions some of the myths that exist about the countryside and explores what it means to sustain an effective Christian presence there. This is followed by six group studies looking at different aspects of this, including ecumenical partnerships and effective presence in the community.

Mike Booker and Mark Ireland, *Evangelism – Which way now?* (London, Church House Publishing, 2003)

This very helpful book evaluates different courses and programmes concerned with the first part of discipleship, the journey to faith. It covers a range of approaches from a variety of theological backgrounds. Booker and Ireland assess courses such as *Alpha, Emmaus - Way of Faith, Credo* and *Start!* as well as considering other approaches such as learning from the world church, community ministry, natural church development and cell church. The book is easy to read and a valuable tool in exploring some of the resources currently available to churches.

Phil Potter, *The Challenge of Cell Church* (Oxford, Bible Reading Fellowship, 2001)

This book explores the potential of small groups and cell church for all churches. The value of *The Challenge of Cell Church* is that it is written from a British perspective and context. Potter draws on his experience at St. Mark's Church, Haydock, to reveal the theory of cell church in practice. Through this he examines the importance of cell values, community, growing cells, evangelism and covenant cells.

It is a practical and easy-to-use resource for any church considering the cell model. Each chapter includes an outline for a small group which explores the challenge of cell through the material just read. The latter chapters look at how to move successfully to a cell church model, and include answers to the five main objections Potter has received. In contrast to other cell church books, Potter doesn't detail the 'prototype' approach of beginning with a single cell, but proposes what he terms the 'big bang', where transition happens in one go.

But it is the final two chapters which will encourage readers to think further about cell. One contains testimonies from cell members of a variety of ages and backgrounds, and the final chapter has an excellent series of cartoons by Ron Bailey, a cell pastor, charting the progress of cells at St. Mark's.

Robert Warren, *The Healthy Churches' Handbook* (London, Church House Publishing, 2004)

Here is a practical guide for churches to identify their strengths, weaknesses and discover what action to take to develop the health of their church. The focus is on the quality of the church's life, not numbers. The book describes a tried and tested process for people to have a conversation about their church (which may be easier for some than talking about their faith). However, people having to think about what the church is doing to nurture their faith and develop their discipleship, means conversations about faith inevitably arise. The book is peppered with examples of what is happening in different churches displaying healthy characteristics - all of which are taking their faith and discipleship seriously, as well as plenty of sound advice for facilitators taking a church through the process.

Leslie Christie, *450 Unfinished Sentences* (Grand Rapids, Zondervan Publishing House, 2000)

This handy pocket-sized book is a brilliant resource for getting young people talking. It is simply a collection of sometimes lighthearted, sometimes poignant, but always provocative unfinished sentences - conversation starters guaranteed to get teenagers talking. They can be used for fun as ice-breakers, or to get people wrestling with deep issues. Examples include: 'I hate it when my parents ... '; 'The thing that scares me most right now is ... '; 'I think the opposite sex has it easiest because ... '; 'Something very few people know about me is ... '; 'Last year at this time I would never have thought God would ... '. They would be pretty good conversation starters among adults too.

Mission-shaped church (London, Church House Publishing, 2004)

This key Anglican report was developed by a working group which included Methodism's Evangelism and Church Planting Secretary. It is helpful for its analysis of contemporary culture and for its considered reflections on a variety of fresh expressions of 'Church', and how some of the experiments have worked out. It explores theology and methodologies for a 'missionary church', and reminds us of the key values of such a church: that it is focused on God the Trinity; that it is incarnational; that it is transformational; that it makes disciples; and that it is relational.

Jeff Proctor-Murphy, David Felten, *Living the questions*

Living the questions is a 12-week DVD and web-based small group study. It describes itself as 'an unapologetically liberal alternative to the *Alpha* course' and seeks to provide a safe place where people have permission to ask the questions they've always wanted to ask about faith, but have been afraid to voice for fear of being thought a heretic.

The sessions include recorded conversations with leading theologians, ministers, sociologists and biblical scholars; sermon and lecture clips; concrete spiritual practices and spiritual disciplines; and suggestions for engagements in acts of social justice. Each session has a particular focus, but ongoing themes explore the nature of biblical authority, the Jesus/Christ dichotomy, and what faith looks like in the 21st century. There is also an extra session on the contribution of Wesleyan theology.

The course material was developed in America by two United Methodist Church pastors, but the list of scholars involved include Leslie Griffiths, and John Bell of the Iona Community. For more information log on to www.livingthequestions.com.

Martin Wray, *Second Wind (Spirituality in the second half of life)*

Launched by M.H.A. at Methodist Conference 2005, *Second Wind* explores the challenges and experiences of later life and how they affect our faith, spiritual growth, relationship with God and the personal quest for inner peace and balance. The six-session programme is designed to include some input, opportunities for sharing of insights and experiences, discussion, prayer and worship. It is intended to be more than simply a study course or discussion group, as group members are asked to pray as well as reflect between meetings. By sharing something of their prayer with the group each week, it should become a real 'spiritual exercise' leading to growth in relationship with God and with one another. For more details, contact MHA (e-mail: spirituality@mha.org.uk).

Our Calling

The calling of the Methodist Church is to respond to the gospel of God's love in Christ and to live out its discipleship in worship and mission.

The Church exists to:

- increase awareness of God's presence and to celebrate God's love ***(Worship)***;
- help people to grow and learn as Christians, through mutual support and care ***(Learning and Caring)***;
- be a good neighbour to people in need and to challenge injustice ***(Service)***;
- make more followers of Jesus Christ ***(Evangelism)***.

(Adopted Conference 2000)

Priorities for the Methodist Church

In partnership with others wherever possible, the Methodist Church will concentrate its prayers, resources, imagination and commitments on this priority:

- To proclaim and affirm its conviction of God's love in Christ, for us and for all the world; and renew confidence in God's presence and action in the world and in the Church

As ways towards realising this priority, the Methodist Church will give particular attention to the following:

- Underpinning everything we do with God-centred worship and prayer;
- Supporting community development and action for justice, especially among the most deprived and poor - in Britain and worldwide;
- Developing confidence in evangelism and in the capacity to speak of God and faith in ways that make sense to all involved;
- Encouraging fresh ways of being Church;
- Nurturing a culture in the Church which is people-centred and flexible.

(Adopted Conference 2004)

Bibliography

- Brian Beck, 'The elusive Methodist identity - who are we?' in ***The Epworth Review*** 27(4) (2000)
- BBC, ICM survey in ***What the World thinks of God,*** broadcast BBC Two, 26th February 2004 (http://news.bbc.co.uk/1/hi/programmes/wtwtgod)
- Madeleine Bunting, ***Willing Slaves - how the overwork culture is ruling our lives*** (London, HarperCollins, 2004)
- Churches Information for Mission, ***Church Life Profile*** (Churches Information for Mission, 2002) (downloadable from www.methodist.org.uk)
- eds. Jane Craske, Clive Marsh, ***Methodism and the Future*** (London, Continuum, 1999)
- Mark Davis, ***Walking on the Shore*** (Chelmsford, Matthew James Publishing Limited, 2002)
- Mark Greene, ***Imagine – How we can reach the UK*** (London, London Institute for Contemporary Christianity/Evangelical Alliance, 2003) (downloadable from www.eauk.org/imagine)
- Mark Greene, ***Supporting Christians at work*** (London, LICC, 2001)
- Hind Working Group (an Anglican body with Methodist and URC representation), ***Education for Discipleship*** (2005)

- Clive Marsh, ***Christianity in a post-atheist age*** (London, SCM Press, 2002)
- eds. Clive Marsh, Brian Beck, Angela Shier-Jones, Helen Wareing, ***Unmasking Methodist Theology***, (London, Continuum, 2004)
- Methodist Church, ***The Methodist Worship Book*** (Peterborough, mph, 1999)
- Methodist Church, ***A Catechism for the use of the people called Methodists*** (Peterborough, mph, 2000)
- Methodist Church, ***The Constitutional Practice and Discipline of the Methodist Church*** (Peterborough, mph, 2004)
- Methodist Conference Agenda, ***Methodist Membership and Christian Discipleship***, Conference 1999
- Methodist Conference Agenda, ***Our Calling,*** Methodist Conference 2000
- Methodist Conference Agenda, ***Learning and Developing as the Whole People of God***, Conference 2001
- Methodist Conference Agenda, ***Priorities for the Methodist Church***, Conference 2004
- Methodist Conference Agenda, ***The Nature of Oversight***, Conference 2005
- Office for National Statistics, ***National Census of 2001*** (http://www.statistics.gov.uk/census2001)
- United Methodist Church, ***The Book of Discipline of the United Methodist Church*** (Nashville, The United Methodist Publishing House, 2004)
- John Wesley, ***A Plain Account of Christian Perfection***

Acknowledgements

Cover image: 'Supper at Emmaus' by Dinah Roe Kendall © Dinah Roe Kendall (1976) from ***Allegories of Heaven: An Artist Explores the 'Greatest Story Ever Told'*** (Piquant, 2002). Used with permission.

Photos: Colin Barrett; Jane Leech; Mark Zaccaria

Quotation from ***The New Revised Standard Version of the Bible*** (Anglicized edition) © 1989, 1985 Division of Christian Education of the National Council of the Churches of Christ in the United States of America. Used by permission. All rights reserved.

Quotations from the Methodist Prayer Handbook 2004-2005, ***Look to Christ*** (Peterborough, mph, 2004), ***The Methodist Worship Book*** (Peterborough, mph, 1999), ***The Constitutional Practice and Discipline of the Methodist Church*** (volume 1) (Peterborough, mph, 1998) (volume 2) (Peterborough, mph, 2004), ***A Catechism for the use of the people called Methodists*** (Peterborough, mph, 2000), ***Methodist Conference Agenda*** (1999, 2000, 2001, 2004, 2005), ***The Epworth Review*** (27(4), 2000), © Trustees for Methodist Church Purposes (TMCP). Used by permission.

eds. Jane Craske, Clive Marsh, ***Methodism and the Future*** (London, Continuum, 1999). Used by permission.

Mark Davis, ***Walking on the Shore*** (Chelmsford, Matthew James Publishing Limited, 2002)

Mark Greene, ***Imagine – How we can reach the UK*** (London, London Institute for Contemporary Christianity/Evangelical Alliance, 2003). Used by permission.

Mark Greene, Mark Greene, ***Supporting Christians at work*** (London, LICC, 2001). Used by permission

eds. Clive Marsh, Brian Beck, Angela Shier-Jones, Helen Wareing, ***Unmasking Methodist Theology***, (London, Continuum, 2004). Used by permission.

Clive Scott, John 1:1-14 revisited. Used by permission

United Methodist Church, ***The Book of Discipline of the United Methodist Church*** (Nashville, The United Methodist Publishing House, 2004)